THE FACE OF
MY PARISH

THE FACE OF MY PARISH

by

TOM ALLAN

HARPER & BROTHERS, PUBLISHERS
New York

Printed in the United States of America

Library of Congress catalog card number: 57-9874

CONTENTS

PREFACE

I undertook the writing of this brief account of the work in my parish with the greatest diffidence. I have no success story to tell. Rather the reverse. Anything I have to say arises, not from the success of the work in North Kelvinside, but from our failure to do anything more than touch the fringes of the problem of serving a predominantly working-class parish in a Glasgow suburb.

I have tried to analyse the causes of our failure in the institutional Church to meet the challenge of secular society, and to set down, as honestly as I am able, the major problems which confronted us as we sought to become a 'missionary parish'. It seems to me that these problems and failures are common to the Church in every situation to-day—whether in a Glasgow suburb, or a new housing area, or a rural community —however much they appear to differ. We make no kind of claim to finding a blue-print for a solution to the problems and an eradication of the failure. We have made some tentative and stumbling steps along a road which has been discovered mainly by the Churches on the Continent and in Asia, and which appears to hold the promise of new life for a Church courageous enough to set out upon it. Increasingly in our own country this road is being followed. What

I have written is an interim report of the first part of the journey.

Since it is an interim report, it is naturally sketchy, hesitant, and probably disjointed. It was written mainly in odd half-hours snatched from the normal unending demands of parish work. At the time of writing this preface, the congregational group has embarked on a long-term mission to the parish, which will put many things which we hold as theories to the test of practice. In a fluid—and often turbulent—situation it is impossible to write an objective and carefully planned appreciation.

I take this opportunity of recording my gratitude to two men who most deeply influenced the course of my ministry in North Kelvinside, and whose guidance and encouragement kept us on the road when we were often tempted to turn aside. First, the Rev. D. P. Thomson, Evangelist of the Church of Scotland, whose Mission in the parish in 1947 began a real movement of the Spirit in our midst. And second, the Rev. R. H. W. Falconer, Religious Broadcasting Organizer for Scotland, whose patience and wisdom led us to recognize the power of the Christian community in evangelism.

I also record my gratitude to the Editor of *The British Weekly* for permission to reprint in this book some material which has appeared in his columns: and to my friend, the Rev. K. J. Turnbull, for preparing the Index.

June 1953   TOM ALLAN

I

THE FACE OF MY PARISH

1. Picture of a Parish

IN George Bernanos' extraordinary book, *The Diary of a Country Priest*, the young priest, coming to his first parish, writes these words in his note-book: ' Just three months to-day since my appointment to this Parish of Ambricourt. Already three months. . . . This morning I prayed hard for my parish, my poor parish, my first and perhaps my last, since I ask no better than to die here. My parish! The words can't even be spoken without a kind of soaring love. . . . But as yet the idea behind them is so confused. I know that my parish is a reality, that we belong to each other for all eternity: it is not a mere administrative fiction, but a living cell in the everlasting Church. But if only the good God would open my eyes and unseal my ears, so that I might behold the face of my parish! The look in the eyes . . . these would be the eyes of all Christianity, of all parishes—perhaps of the poor human race itself. Our Lord saw them from the Cross. . . .'

When I think of the parish to which I was sent to minister seven years ago, these words always come into my mind. In Scotland to-day there is a tendency to dismiss the parish as an administrative or geographical fiction. We are constantly being told that the parish

9

system has broken down, especially in urban communities. Can it have broken down because not many of us are able to regard it as a ' living cell in the everlasting Church ' ? Or because we look upon it as so many streets and houses, forgetting that our parish is a community of living people for whom God has made us responsible ? Perhaps the parish in Scotland —and elsewhere—will continue to be an administrative fiction until we have learned to pray over it like Bernanos' priest, and ask the good Lord to let us see its face and hear its voice.

I can still remember with great vividness the terror which took hold of me the first time I walked round my parish in September 1946. It seemed as if there was not love, but hostility, between us. I felt that all the windows were eyes looking into my soul and seeing the emptiness there. Where did one begin in such a situation ? It was not long before the problems became articulate and well defined—and completely overwhelming.

The Parish of North Kelvinside is typical of so many city parishes—and typical, in some ways, of the city itself. It covers an area of something like a square mile in the north-west of Glasgow, and is completely built up. Into that square mile a population of nearly ten thousand souls is crowded, mainly in four-storey tenements—there are close on two thousand homes. There is a considerable variety of housing conditions, and the people in the parish represent a fair cross-section of the population of the city. On the north side the houses are mostly room-and-kitchen or ' single-end ', desperately overcrowded, and marked by all the worst features of Victorian working-class tenement building. In the centre of the parish, immediately around the church, there are more recently built three-roomed flats housing mainly the ' white-collar ' workers. And in the west, overlooking the banks of the River Kelvin and the Botanic Gardens, there are the more spacious flats of the professional classes.

There are no new houses of any kind in the parish, and no room for building. During the past five years, with the housing expansion on the outskirts of the city, there has been a slight shift of population among the larger working-class families. But with the housing situation in the city so acutely difficult, there is no possibility of depopulation for many years to come. On the whole it is a stable community.

The church is strategically situated in the centre of the parish. It was built at the end of the last century to meet the needs of the growing community, beginning its history as an ' extension charge ' of the United Presbyterian Church.

At the very outset I was to realize that there was only the most tenuous bond between the parish and the parish church. In a parish of ten thousand souls, in 1946 the communicant membership of North Kelvinside stood at just over four hundred; and of that number perhaps a quarter lived within the actual bounds of the parish itself. Out of nearly two thousand homes less than a hundred claimed a connection with their parish church.

It was small comfort to realize that this is quite typical of the problem with which the Church is faced in every part of Britain to-day. A recent and reliable statistical survey of church life in Scotland claims that only 56 per cent of the adult population are communicant members of a church—and that figure includes Roman Catholics. During these past seven years the work of evangelism has taken me to most types of parish in this country. And I have no reason to doubt that the figures quoted for church attendance in the Anglican report *Towards the Conversion of England* give an accurate account of the situation. About 15 per cent of the people regularly attend a place of worship: probably about 30 per cent go on some special occasion: some 40-50 per cent are quite indifferent to religion: and the remaining 10 per cent are hostile.

The challenging fact which emerges from these figures is not that we are faced in this country with any degree of hostility to the Church, or that we are on the defensive against a militant and vociferous paganism. It is something much more subtle and difficult to deal with—simply that the vast majority of people regard the Church as irrelevant. 'The influence which the Church once had on the nation has diminished,' says Dr. Garbett in his book *In an Age of Revolution*, 'religion is now the concern of a small section of its people; its claim for the whole of life is no longer made with any confidence, and only very rarely treated as serious.'

Such a judgment is bound to disturb the most complacent. In 1946 I had a glimpse of my parish, not as a living cell in the everlasting Church, but as a broken, divided, inchoate mass of people with no centre for their community and no centre for their lives; the church on their doorstep was quite irrelevant for most of them.

I remember, near the beginning of my ministry, a lad from the parish coming to me and asking me to officiate at his wedding. I asked him about his church connection. Frankly, and without any sense of embarrassment, he told me he had none—that he had not been inside a church, except for church parades in the army, since he was a child. I asked him to tell me honestly why he didn't go to church. It was obvious that the question was new to him and that he had never thought about it before. Finally he replied: ' I believe in God: isn't that enough? '

Amusing? Or tragic? The significant thing about his reply was surely this: that even his belief in God—naïve and superficial it may have been—was entirely unconnected with the building at the corner of the street which he passed every day on his way to work. For him—and for hundreds like him in my parish—the Church is irrelevant.

Then, at the beginning of things, I knew what the French priest-workman Father Dillard meant when he wrote: ' What was I to do? What was I to say to them? I felt that I was a stranger to them—that I belonged to another culture. My liturgy, my theology, my prayers, my priestly dress—all cut me off from them and made me a being apart. Can Christ have lost his power of attracting or the strength that he is able to communicate to others? Or are we at the end of time, when charity hardly exists on the earth? Am I—with a handful of those like me—an isolated being—one who has found the pearl of great price, and has to keep the secret to himself? Is France a country to be abandoned to her fate? '

Perhaps it is good that they cannot tell us of this kind of despair in our theological colleges. We have to discover it for ourselves.

2. *The Task of the Ministry*

This situation which I have tried to describe is no different from that which faces most ministers as they go to their first charge. They find themselves ministering to a congregation separated by a seemingly impassable barrier from the community in which it is expected to bear its witness. And the question which has to be answered is simply: how can this congregation begin to fulfil the function for which it was created? How can this church become in fact—and not only in theory—the Body of Christ in this community? How can its gospel be communicated to men and women who apparently feel no need of it?

Daniel Jenkins underlines the problem in his book, *The Gift of the Ministry*, and points to one of the glaring weaknesses of modern Protestantism. He writes: ' In such a situation it is clear that before we can hope to achieve successful communication we must realize how difficult it is and how great an effort it demands. The Church has partly failed to see this in modern times, almost until the present day, because in Anglo-Saxon Protestantism at least, she has been dazzled by the cult of the " popular preacher ". This was, of course, a feature chiefly of late Victorian and Edwardian days . . . and it still affects the way in which we conceive of how communication between minister and people should effectively be made. . . . What we must deliver ourselves from is the notion expressed by many enthusiastic spirits in these days, that the gospel is not triumphantly spread abroad because we fail to " sell " it effectively enough, and that all that we need is to be more energetic, dynamic, up-to-date and super-efficient.

The task is a difficult one and we are almost certain to be performing it badly if we go forward under the illusion that it is likely to be easy.'

I quote this extensively not only because it realistically emphasizes the difficulty of the problem of communication in the widest sense, but also because it diagnoses a disease from which our Church suffers. It seems to me that our theological training, for example, regards it as axiomatic that every man leaving college has the human gifts to make a 'popular' preacher, and that that type of ministry is—perhaps unconsciously— the standard by which a successful ministry is judged. It is a fact that, in many branches of the Reformed Church, success or failure is very largely dependent on the personality of the incumbent, and the man who has not been gifted with those human qualities which appear to draw people to him is compelled to resign himself to a pedestrian ministry which leaves the secular community around largely unmarked and unconcerned.

Surely our supreme need is to discover some pattern of life in our Church through which the gospel may be communicated to needy men and women—*a pattern independent of personal qualities and qualifications.* To this end a great deal of thought and study is being directed in the Church to-day. After three years' deliberations a special Commission of the General Assembly of the Church of Scotland reported in these terms: 'The Commission feels that our time demands a fresh emphasis on the importance of the parochial principle for the life and service of the Church . . . the adequate fulfilment by the Church of its national responsibility depends upon the efficient working of the parochial system, but there is grave reason to question how far this condition is being fulfilled. . . . One way or another the situation must be faced, and effective steps taken to the end that the parochial system be not merely a traditional institution which has largely lost its significance, but an effective instrument for the present spread of the Gospel influence.'

All of which, to a man beginning his ministry, appeared to be very true. It is one thing, however, to be told that the parish system must become 'effective' if the Church is to fulfil its national responsibility. It is quite another thing to be saddled with a working-class parish in Glasgow, and make it as effective for the spread of the gospel influence as the Commission so sincerely desires.

At the simplest level, there is the mere question of physical resources. Even with a congregation of just over four hundred I found my days more than fully occupied. My meagre resources were exhausted trying to cope with the clamorous demands of my own congregation, and the ten thousand dwellers in my parish might as well have lived at the other side of the world for all that I could see of them.

One apparent solution to the dilemma is a team ministry. It remains only a theoretical possibility as far as the Church of Scotland is concerned—whether or not it would meet the demands of the situation. There is neither the man-power nor the financial resources even to experiment with the idea.

What then? Does the gap between the church and its parish remain unbridged? Do we resign ourselves to the impossibility of implementing the recommendations of committees, and let the missionary work of the Church take a secondary place? If we believe that Christ is Lord not only of the Church but of the world, and that the Church is his Body, the agent and instrument of his redemptive purpose, where do we begin? Is it possible to find some method of approach, some pattern of life and witness by which the gospel is to be communicated?

It was in 1947—at the beginning of the second year of my ministry—that something happened which set in motion a movement within my congregation and parish which is still in progress at the time of writing, and which we believe is leading us towards an answer.

The work of the Rev. D. P. Thomson is widely known in Scotland and beyond. For thirty years he has been an evangelist, and since the war he has been Evangelist of the Church of Scotland's Home Board. I do not know any man who has given himself so unsparingly to the work of the Kingdom during these years. Hundreds of people throughout Scotland to-day owe their Christian faith to his ministry. Scores of ministers, like myself, have looked to him for guidance and inspiration. Prior to the war he was engaged mainly in evangelism on traditional lines, using teams of ministers and students in brief campaigns within an area. The experience of a post-war campaign in the borders led him to see the possibilities of what had become known as 'visitation evangelism', in which the main feature of the mission is the house-to-house visitation of the parish or district.

In the summer of 1947 Mr. Thomson suggested that North Kelvinside might be used as the centre for an experiment in visitation evangelism. The parish was ideally situated to such an experiment. It was compact and accessible. It had a great variety of housing conditions. The church was conveniently and centrally situated. Accordingly plans were made to carry out a door-to-door visitation of the parish in the autumn of that year.

That Mission marked a turning point in my own ministry. Its results in both congregation and parish were more far-reaching than we could have envisaged. But it has been a painful business. Perhaps if we had known what lay ahead we would never have undertaken it.

II

EXPERIMENT IN PAROCHIAL EVANGELISM

I. Plan of Campaign

AT the beginning of the second year of my ministry things looked fairly successful. New members were coming in. The numbers at the Sunday services were slowly increasing, and the week-night organizations were in good shape. But I had no illusions about the apparent success. It left the major problems unanswered. Worse than that—it offered an attractive distraction from their challenge. Two things kept thrusting themselves in front of me, however. The first was that within my own congregation there was little sign of any significant deepening of spiritual life. And it was still painfully obvious that the ordinary life of the congregation was still totally divorced from the life of the community round its doors.

It was a situation which offered excellent scope for an experiment in visitation evangelism. At the beginning of a ministry there is little in the way of opposition from the membership to any new scheme which is not going to impose any great demands on them. There will be more to say about that later. And so, when the Rev. D. P. Thomson outlined his plan to the Kirk Session it was received—if not with enthusiasm—at least with friendly tolerance.

There is nothing new in the technique of house-to-house visitation in parochial evangelism. The seventy disciples whom Jesus sent out two by two were probably doing something very similar to what has become known as ' visitation evangelism '. I know of a parish minister in the West of Scotland who carried out a campaign of this kind at the turn of the present century. And since the union of the Churches in Scotland in 1929 it has become a method of evangelism strongly recommended by the Home Mission Committee. The Iona Community have laid great emphasis on the importance of it, and it had been carried out with signal success in a variety of different parishes. In America, as one would expect, the technique of visitation evangelism has been worked out in the past thirty years with devastating thoroughness.

There was, however, one important difference in the method of D. P. Thomson's campaign in North Kelvinside. It would have been impossible for me to recruit a team to carry out the visitation of the parish from my own membership. It was a venture into unknown territory which even the most devoted church workers viewed with much trepidation and concern. And even if volunteers from the membership of the congregation had been forthcoming they would have had neither the training nor the equipment to do more than pay a friendly call on the people round their doors. The significant factor in our parish mission was that the initial visitation was carried out by a team of volunteers from outside the parish itself, drawn from the personnel who had been engaged in the work of seaside missions under Mr. Thomson's leadership.

The visiting team numbered some fifty men and

women. Of these five were ministers, twelve were divinity students, thirteen were students of other faculties, and the remainder were young men and women from business and industry. The campaign was planned to last for a fortnight, Saturdays and Sundays excepted for visitation. It meant that two thousand homes had to be visited in ten weekdays.

This can be nothing more than a bald statement of facts. To catch the authentic spirit of mission which pervaded these ten extraordinary days one had to live through them. And even at the time we were not fully aware of all that was happening both in the church and in the parish. The years which have followed have served to bring to light many significant things which were not apparent in the middle of the experience.

The campaign began on a Sunday in the middle of September, when Mr. Thomson preached at the morning service, meeting the elders, managers, and Sunday school teachers after the service. On the Monday night, and each weekday during the Mission, operations began at quarter past five with a meeting for prayer in the church. At six o'clock the team sat down to tea in the church hall, and this fellowship meal played an important part in the Mission, as we were to discover. The briefing of the visitors, and their allocation in the parish followed.

It was left to each individual to decide whether he wanted to do the visitation alone, or in company with another member of the team, and generally half the team visited singly and half in pairs. There are advantages in both methods. Some people are shy and inarticulate in the presence of another worker. Others prefer the moral support of company. Each visitor carried a note-book and pencil, a letter from the minister to the people of the parish, and a selection of the Church's literature for sale in the course of the visitation.

About seven o'clock each evening the visitors set out. The aims of the visitation, outlined by Mr. Thomson, were these: (i) To carry the greetings of the Church to every home in the parish, irrespective of congregational or denominational tie. (ii) To gather as much information as possible about the family and church connection in each home. (iii) To bring something of the wealth and variety of the Church's literature to those who never had either the time or the opportunity to see it. (iv) Where no vital church connection existed (and only in such cases) to extend an invitation to the parish church, and to suggest that a follow-up visit might be made by a representative of that church. (v) To make a natural witness for Christ, and do such personal work as circumstances might permit or suggest.

Towards nine o'clock the visitors began to return to the church hall, where their reports were taken, and the information they had gathered transferred to index cards. Gradually a statistical account of the parish began to emerge, and at the end of each evening a list of homes which called for a follow-up visit was compiled. Supper and prayers ended the work of the evening.

On the next evening, while the visiting team continued to make the initial contacts in the parish, a small and very fearful group of North Kelvinside members began the work of follow-up—a handful of elders, Sunday school teachers and members of the Women's Guild—volunteering for this work more out of loyalty than anything else.

We shall go on to examine the lessons and discoveries of this Mission. But here is one story which came out of it which may point the way forward. A member of the congregation has a small shop in the parish—in the most densely populated part of it. The week following the Mission a regular customer came in to the shop. She asked an unusual question. 'Are you?' she said to the shop-keeper, 'a member of that church down the road?' The shop-keeper admitted membership. 'Well,' said the customer, 'you can't think much of your church. I've been coming in here day in and day out for twenty-five years, and you've never thought to ask me to a service. But I'm starting next Sunday.' To-day the customer—out of the Church for years— is in her place twice a Sunday. And the shop-keeper? She understands more clearly what it means to be a member of the Church of Jesus Christ.

2. *Lessons and Discoveries of Visitation*

In his book, *The Practice of Evangelism*, Canon Bryan Green writes: 'I am sure we shall approach any study of methods of evangelism from a false standpoint unless we realize from the outset that many methods have been born out of the travail of a soul. Any picture of a group of Christians sitting calmly down to draw up a blue-print for evangelism . . . gives an entirely wrong impression. Rather we must picture Christians thinking, praying, and struggling to find a way, and out of that spiritual experience is discovered . . . an adaptation of some well-tried method which is baptized afresh by the Spirit who is guiding them.'

The Mission of house-to-house visitation which had

just been completed in my parish was not the working out of a carefully prepared plan of campaign. It was a halting and tentative experiment carried out by a team of people who had never done this kind of work before, and within a church which had neither a previous experience of this method of evangelism nor any great enthusiasm for it. And yet—for my own congregation at least—an adaptation of this well-tried method was assuredly baptized by the Holy Spirit.

Within ten weekdays the visiting team had called on 1,854 homes in the parish, and the small group of volunteers from my own congregation were in the middle of the follow-up work. At that point we were able to take stock, and set down at least the immediate results of the campaign.

First of all, a great deal of valuable information was recorded regarding the religious life of the parish. Here are the statistics:

Homes with no church connection	667
Homes with Roman Catholic connection	328
Homes connected with North Kelvinside (the parish church)	116
Homes connected with other Protestant churches (or missions)	743
	1,854

These figures speak for themselves. For one thing they re-emphasized the nature of the problem, and shattered any remnants of complacency which were left in me. A theory regarding the irrelevance of the

Church was translated into hard facts. I could not escape the challenge of this—that nearly forty per cent of the homes round the door of my church were entirely unconnected with any place of Christian worship. At the same time, however, these figures helped to reduce a superhuman problem to one of recognizable and manageable proportions. Six months before the Mission began the people in my parish were strangers to me. I knew nothing about them—the size of the family, the conditions under which they were living, their church affiliations—all this was unknown territory. At the end of the Mission a new situation existed. I had a record of every home in the parish. I knew those which were Roman Catholic, those which claimed connection with a Protestant church or mission. And, most important, I had a precise index of all those homes which had become separated from the Church. These were my first responsibility.

The second immediate result of the Mission was reflected in the life of the congregation itself. Within the space of three months close on a hundred new members were added to the Communion roll—half of them by profession of faith, and half either by restoration of a lapsed membership or by what we call in Scotland 'transfer of certificate'. Many of these certificates of membership which were handed to me were from churches in all parts of the country. Many of them were dated fifteen or twenty years before. I can never forget the service of confirmation following the Mission. We were careful not to press any individual to come forward into full membership. A long and rigorous course of instruction awaited those who did come. They were people of all types and ages and backgrounds. And as they stood at the confirmation service to make their profession of faith it was a moving sight. An old couple in their seventies who had not been inside a church since the day of their marriage forty years before stood beside a boy in his teens. Parents and their children stood together. I began to see the meaning of the missionary Church, and realized for the first time the compelling power of the redeemed community.

In many other parts of the congregation's life the effects of the Mission were immediately felt. Within a month the Sunday school was exactly doubled, and every organization showed an increase. Attendances at public worship began to rise, and this brought a considerable increase in congregational liberality.

These were the tangible results of the Mission. But they were by no means the most important results. Already, within a few weeks of the end of the Mission, certain significant things were becoming evident. On three separate groups of people it made a powerful impact. First, on those in the parish living outside the fellowship of the Church. The visitors were amazed at the friendliness of the response which they received as they went from door to door. In ten homes out of all those visited they were met with a shut door. In the others they were received not merely with courtesy but with marked interest. The Roman Catholic homes were among the friendliest in the parish. Over and over again the response was the same. 'We're glad you've come,' people would say. 'We have wanted to get back to the Church, but we didn't know how to go about it . . . can we start now?' The gulf between the Church and the parish was beginning to be bridged.

And even among those who showed no inclination to return to the Church an interest was created which was at least a step forward from the bland indifference of a former day.

An equally profound impact was made on those few members of the congregation who volunteered to take part in the work of follow-up. As the nights of the Mission passed it was a thrilling thing to see how that handful of people were transformed, and to see how they communicated their enthusiasm to other members of the congregation. At the time Dr. John Foster did a broadcast about it, in which he said : ' I heard something unusual was going on in a Glasgow church recently . . . I found it quite an adventure, and by the look of them so did the young folk engaged in it. It was a joy to see their keenness and efficiency . . . the follow-up had begun before the pioneer stage was completed, so I was able to see not only these young men and women reporting, but some of the church elders come back. " How did you get on ? " asked the minister. " Had a grand time at the first house," said the elder. You could see he was simply bubbling over with it. " He had all sorts of arguments against religion, so I said : ' I can't answer all that, but our minister is going to preach about that very thing on Sunday. Will you come and give him a sporting chance ? ' " Over and over again they found old links with the Church, here or elsewhere, which were still something very precious . . . I went home that night feeling something of a thrill. Here was a church busy as it could be, and about the Lord's business; not money-raising efforts, or merely keeping church machinery going—but getting into relationship with people outside and bringing

people into touch with God.'   When the Mission ended
I could count on a score of people within my own
congregation whose eyes had been opened to the meaning of their membership in the Church, and who saw
for the first time an avenue of service which they had
never realized was there.

There was a third group of people upon whom the
Mission made its own impact.   These were the members of the congregation who took no part in it.   I
believe that their reactions to this kind of parochial
effort are determinative and decisive, and I want to
examine these reactions now in some detail.

3. Tension and Conflict

In a congregation with a nominal membership of
just over four hundred, I have said that about twenty
took an active part in the work of the Mission.   The
others stood on the sidelines and watched the work
going on. These onlookers exist in every church. They
form the overwhelming majority of the membership,
and not infrequently occupy the main posts in the
administration of the local church's institutional life.
Their influence in the life and witness of the church
is not always in proportion to their spiritual understanding.   They are the conventional church members
who are, on the whole, perfectly content with things
as they are.   Within this group in my own church the
Visitation Campaign produced a threefold reaction.

Many of them remained completely unconcerned
with all that was going on.   For them the church exists
as a place of worship on a Sunday—once a Sunday—
and they remain stubbornly impervious both to the

normal organizational life of the church and to any attempt to widen its sphere of influence. They are not hostile—they are merely indifferent.

A second group within the onlookers found themselves confronted with an entirely new situation the challenge of which they could not avoid. They had listened to sermons on the responsibility of the layman to witness to his faith. They probably agreed in principle with everything that was said. They were good church folk with a genuine love for their church, and prepared to give their time and service to the conventional pattern of its life. They would work for a bazaar, collect money for a new boiler, organize a bus outing, sing in the choir, even teach a Sunday school class. That was within the area of church life known to them and accepted by them. But the thought of their having a part to play in the work of evangelism was new to them. They were suspicious of the very word 'evangelism'. Was it not connected with the Salvation Army and the Mission Hall? They were sceptical about ordinary people who made any kind of profession of being a 'Christian'. If you asked them, they would disclaim the title, saying they were by no means good enough to be called Christians. Are they not the back-bone of every congregation in our churches to-day—good, sincere people for whom the dynamic of a personal faith is an unknown and rather frightening thing?

It was fascinating to watch the reaction of these people first of all to the work of the team which came to do the initial visitation, and secondly to the members of North Kelvinside who began slowly to help with the follow-up. Gradually the barriers were broken down.

Imperceptibly their attitude began to change, and over the years it continued to change. They are no longer sceptical about those who call themselves Christians. If they themselves have not made the great decision, and laid hold on the faith of Christ as their own, at least they look wistfully at those who know this experience, and in moments when the barriers are down, long to have it for themselves. If they are not yet committed to the work of evangelism in their own parish, at least they realize its necessity, and help to forward it by their interest and often by their practical help. If they do not feel that they can go out on visitation, for example, many of them will do clerical work, preparing cards, taking reports, compiling lists. And they will watch for the stranger in church and offer him a welcome. Probably the most far-reaching results of the first Mission have been seen in the lives of the men and women and young people in this group. From it has come some of the best workers in succeeding years. And, as I hope to show, with this group lies the key to evangelism in the present situation.

There was, however, a third group among the onlookers; and it is with the people in this group that I am mainly concerned at this stage. They are those incredible people who—while they must at some time have taken solemn vows of membership in the Church after due and proper instruction—have apparently either forgotten the vows they took or have succeeded in living in a state of total illusion during their whole church life. They are of the type of elder who in my own congregation characterized house-to-house visitation as ' religious commercial travelling '. They are of the type of member of long standing who said to a friend of mine—an eminent minister in Edinburgh—when he called at her home: 'Mr. —, I don't like your preaching. I have been a member of the church in which you are now unfortunately the minister for thirty-five years, and I want to tell you that I strongly object to being called a sinner.'

Of course we laugh at those things. It is as well that we can laugh at them, or some of us might have been tempted to give up the ministry long ago. They are symbols of an attitude of mind more common than many of us care to admit among our church people—an attitude of mind which is implacably opposed to any change in the routine of conventional religion, and which sets itself against any effort to confront a congregation with its missionary responsibility.

The Mission of Visitation in North Kelvinside opened up new fields of service for a great many people. It also provided the occasion of tension and conflict.

The experience in my own parish has been duplicated wherever I have gone in the work of evangelism. The main line of opposition to mission in Scotland does not come from the pagan masses outside the Church. By and large they have been ready to listen to the gospel, and have received our witness, whether in visitation or in public meetings or at the street-corner or in the factory, both with courtesy and interest. By far the most bewildering conflict arises within the Church, when the demands of Christ upon his people are heard by those for whom religion is a matter of comfortable and respectable conformity.

The opposition in my own church was confined to a tiny minority, and continued to be inarticulate and underground. Of course, it was there. A member of the congregation suggested that the church could never be the same for her again. When she came to worship on a Sunday she felt a complete stranger, with so many people around her whom she had never met. It was a sad day when the church opened its doors to these people.

The devastating thing about this sort of conflict within the church is that it cannot be concealed from those who are finding their way back, after years outside. And this, more than anything else, is the reason for the extraordinary situation which exists to-day, when men are showing a new interest in—almost a hunger for— the things of the Faith, and at the same time a terrifying indifference to the Church. Melville Chaning-Pearce writes in his book, *The Deep Church*: 'The tide of a return to a religious life-attitude has long been flowing. For generations the Church has seen no such hunger and thirst for the gospel as beats upon all her frontiers to-day. It is only equalled, for such as these, by a no less violent repulsion from churchianity in all its aspects.' An overstatement? Not in my experience. And this repulsion will continue to exist so long as there are people within our churches for whom mission is a disreputable business and not the very reason for the Church's existence.

4. *The Problem of Assimilation*

In the months following the Mission I was to learn a shocking but salutary lesson. I had been concerned to discover some answer to the problem of winning the non-churchgoing masses round my door into the sphere of the Church's work and witness. This I was to learn from the Mission of Visitation—that it is the easiest thing in the world to get people to 'join' the Church; it is supremely difficult to know what to do with them once they are in; and it is virtually impossible to keep the majority of them within the conventional framework of the Church's life.

Within two years of the Mission of Visitation I found that the congregation had exactly doubled itself. In 1950, at the time of the Glasgow Churches Campaign, when we carried out another door-to-door visitation of the parish, the process of nominal addition began again. And in five and a half years we saw the accession of more than eight hundred new members, most of them from the immediate environs of the church.

The solution of one problem, however, left me with another—and far greater—problem on my hands. It might be called the problem of assimilation. In the course of the years following the Mission I discovered that, far from being the minister of a growing congregation, I was in fact in danger of becoming the minister of two congregations, worshipping in the same building, and called by the same name, but separate in every other sense. There were those who had grown up in the church and had worshipped in it all their days. And there were those who had been brought in through the campaigns of visitation, some of them lapsed members of other churches, the majority of them working-class men and women who had come forward by profession of faith. Tragically we had to watch many of these people drifting away as the months passed from a church which appeared to have nothing for them and which was incapable of assimilating them into its life. Of course a great number of them remained. Their

names are still on the roll. They come to Communion
from time to time. But only a small proportion of them
have been won into the full life of the Church. And
we are forced to ask ourselves why.

The answer to that question not only takes us to the
heart of the problem of evangelism in the modern situation; it compels us to re-examine the fundamental presuppositions which govern all our thinking about the
nature, function, and pattern of the Church. Why
should there be any difficulty of assimilation? Why
should it be such a heartbreaking task to bring new
members into the full life of Christian fellowship within our churches? Why do so many of those who have
been won for the Church in campaigns of visitation and
other evangelistic efforts so often drift away? It seems
to me that there are three answers at least to these
questions.

First of all, it is a plain fact that a great number of
the newcomers are simply chilled out of the church by
the attitude of the old members. I know that this is
superficial and a completely unworthy reason for anyone to give for leaving a church. But it exists, and has
to be taken soberly into account. Here is a woman
who, since the time of her marriage, twenty years
before, has lost the habit of churchgoing. When she
was a girl she lived in a country village, attended church
with her whole family, came to her first Communion
as a matter of social custom and with complete sincerity. After her marriage she comes to live in the city,
goes through the bitter, desperate years of the early
thirties with a family growing up round about her,
knows what poverty is, and hunger. Her neighbours
never go to church, have no time for it, regard it as

something for the bosses. But one night she is called
upon by two girls from the parish church. She sees in
them a picture of herself twenty years before. She
wants to go back. Can we understand what it means
for that woman to go into church again? It is not easy
to make a decision like that, especially when the
decision involves taking a step which singles her out
from her own social group. She comes to a service in
North Kelvinside, and happens to sit in the seat of that
very person who, God help us, asks her to move. Can
we blame her for not coming back? Has this woman
no heart to feel the insult? You can be certain that it
will take more than a Mission of Visitation to bring her
again into the so-called fellowship of Christ's people.

The second reason for our failure to assimilate the
new member into the full life of the church lies, I
believe, in the hopeless inadequacy of our 'non-Sab-
batical' activities within the church itself. When a
man has been moved to join himself again to a church
after a lapse of years there must be two things at least
in his mind. For one thing he is impressed by the fact
that his parish church is taking the trouble to come and
find him, and imagines that it must be a living and vital
community to undertake such an effort. In other
words, he takes us literally. And secondly, this man's
return to the church is unlikely to be made out of
mere conventionalism. Over and over again I have
found that he is genuinely concerned to meet the
demands of service which he imagines the church is
going to make upon him. But what, in fact, have we
to offer him, apart from the Sunday services? He might
sing in the choir, if he can sing. Obviously he is not
at the stage of teaching a Sunday school class. It is

unlikely that he will be called on to bear office in the church either as manager or elder until years have passed. If there is a Men's Association or Club we might teach him to play carpet bowls, or let him listen to a discussion on politics or look at a film of someone's holiday in Switzerland, or sing Scots' songs at the Burns' Supper. And beyond that? Time and again I have seen men lost to the Church—usually the kind of people we want most to have with us—simply because we have nothing to offer them. Of course we talk in our sermons about Christian service. But are we honestly making any kind of effort to translate our words into action, and provide for our people some sphere in which their sincere desire for service can be made real? We are constantly asking why there are so few men in the Church. Might it not be because we can only appoint a certain number of office-bearers?

These two reasons for our failure to assimilate the newcomers are not, however, decisive. They are only symptomatic of a much deeper malaise with which we are afflicted in the Church to-day, and which, mercifully, we are beginning to understand. 'The answer is,' says Godin in his book, *France Pagan?*, 'that the parish and the proletarian worlds are not merely separated, they are also utterly different. Parochial Christianity, reconstituted in France during the birth of the middle classes, possesses its own culture: catholic, of course, but soaked through with a bourgeois mentality, coloured by bourgeois qualities and by bourgeois defects. A great preoccupation with what is "respectable", a concern with refinement in appearance and speech, a sense of order, good administration, well-run accounts, a certain good taste. . . .' It is my profound belief that this cleavage between the Church and the world, so apparent in the pagan secularism of France, is no less real in our own country, however much we try to disclaim it, and delude ourselves into thinking that we still possess in Britain the pattern of a Christian culture.

And here is the irony of the situation. It is not as if the separation between the Church and the world, which makes it so hard to achieve any common place of meeting, is in fact the separation between the Christian 'style of life' and its secular opposite. It is, rather, a cleavage between two types of secularism. The only difference is that the secularism of the Church retains the tattered remnants of a Christian background.

This, it seems to me, is the main reason for our failure to assimilate new members into the full fellowship of the Church—this cleavage which exists between the Church and the world from which these people have come. We may delude ourselves into thinking that the vast majority of people have rejected the Church because they no longer accept what we might call a 'religious life-attitude'. It is my own conviction that nothing could be further from the truth. They reject the Church because it represents another type of secular culture diametrically opposed to their own. And if we are genuinely concerned to see the barriers between the gospel and the world destroyed we have to examine seriously and honestly the profound defects and anomalies which exist within that community divinely ordained as the channel of communication. The main reason for our ineffectiveness in combating the secularism of the world is that we ourselves in the Church have capitulated to secularism of another kind.

III

THE CHURCH WITHIN
THE CHURCH

1. The Secular Church

THE pungent analysis of the situation in Paris which
the Abbé Godin made in his book, *France Pagan?*, seems
to me to be completely valid for my own parish. He
wrote: 'It is not merely anarchists, or fallen girls, or
professional boxers who cannot be integrated into a
parochial community. It is the people of Paris as a
whole—educated as they have been with no trace of
Christianity. It is the fashionable dressmakers. It is
Renault's foreman. It is M. Dupuy living most respect-
ably in his childless home, which is very elegant and
the type of an honourable pagan establishment. It is
the artisan who has saved up a little money and
acquired a little culture but has once and for all " judged
the Church ", as he will tell you, and has found her
wanting and will not go back upon his judgment. It is
the engineer who has just come in to mend my telephone and who had enough curiosity to talk to me for
a little while, but who feels infinitely remote from the
Christian community of the neighbourhood. It is
almost every man we know in our regiment—and in
the regiments of many of our fellow-priests—who will
never become Christians by joining a group that they
cannot help looking on as a world apart. . . .'

There is a tendency in our own country to imagine that the gulf separating the Church and the world is not so wide as it has obviously become in France. Be that as it may, it is evident that we have no room for complacency. My own church offered a clear illustration. Situated as it is in the middle of a predominantly working-class community, I found when I became its minister that its membership was drawn largely from outside its own parish, and that only a handful of families round its doors were connected with it. And what happened to these people when they did come in? One of two things. Either they remained on the circumference of the congregation's life; or by their very membership in the church they became separated from their social group. They became 'respectable', different from the people among whom they lived, and separated from them, not by their Christian profession, but by their assimilation of a superimposed middle-class culture. The common reason given so often in city parishes for non-churchgoing—we meet with it on every campaign of house-to-house visitation—that they 'have no decent clothes to wear', is symptomatic of the social distinctions which have divorced the churchgoing people among the working-classes from their neighbours living in the same tenement, symptomatic of the cleavage between two cultures. One of the leading evangelists in France expressed it like this: "The embourgeoisement of the churches has gone so far that, except in certain vital and progressive ventures and among the Pentecostals or the Salvation Army, the proletariat have deserted the churches, or else by staying in the churches they have deserted their class.'

In a recent booklet, published by the Secretariat for

Evangelism of the World Council of Churches, on
Evangelism in France, there is a penetrating study of
this *bourgeois* ' culture pattern ' which goes to the heart
of the matter.   And although the writer reminds us that
his study is based on an examination of the contempor-
ary French *bourgeoisie*, and should not be given too
generalized an application, everything that he says
corresponds with my own convictions and experience.
He asserts that ' the *bourgeois* chief expectations in life
are stability and security; he is the sworn enemy of all
change which would involve any risk . . . he is a man
with a safe bank account and a life insurance policy.
(He) strives to perpetuate the established order of things
which has, for him, by the mere fact of its existence,
a sacred connotation. . . . His attitude towards the
Christian faith and the Church is naturally determined
by this overall pattern.   The bourgeois is keenly interested in religion in so far as it may be of assistance to
his quest for respectability . . . he is willing to listen
to the gospel so long as he is able to discern in its
message a morale-building force. . . .'

How does the secularism of the Church express
itself?   The booklet which I have just quoted goes
on to describe the relevant features in the prevailing
pattern of the conventional Church's life.   These
are :

' An *enclosed* community life; the doors are only
open to the " outsider " (what a bourgeois word!) if and
when he has proved his willingness to accept without
question the entire code of recognized rules, though the
Biblical foundation and even the Christian relevance of
these rules may be doubtful.

' A long and painful process of acculturation must be undergone before it is possible really to "belong" to a church.

' A constant effort on the part of the church to prove its "respectability" . . . we are grateful to every sinner who repents, but we really rejoice in every close association of our church with "good" families and "leaders".

' An ardent desire for self-perpetuation : reforms are easily labelled "revolutions". Most of the available resources are used for the maintenance of an acquired position, and almost everyone takes this for granted.

' A complacency in accepting "an adjectival rôle in the life of the nation", the latter being regarded as the "substantive reality".

' A frequent disguise of mere sentimental philanthropy by high-sounding slogans about social justice.

' Introversion and allophoby.'

I have not come across any description which more aptly describes that process of secularization so evident in the Church to-day. The 'enclosed community life' is a fact which there is no disguising, and this enclosed community is dominated by a set of values and characterized by a range of 'activities' whose only authority or justification is that they are traditional. The respectability, the desire for self-perpetuation, the complacency, above all the introversion and allophoby—are not these the familiar marks of so much of the Church's life in our own country?

The secularism of the Church has not only produced a culture pattern which separates it from the mass of the people. It has resulted in something far more bewildering. It has so compromised the message of the New Testament to fit in with its own standards that the gospel proclaimed by this Church is not regarded as a serious alternative to the rival ideologies which are bidding to-day for the allegiance of men. In other words, the Church is separated from the working-classes by its subservience to a *bourgeois* culture; and it is separated from the intellectuals by its apparent dishonesty. It has transformed the revolutionary ethic of Jesus into an inoffensive prudential morality. It has watered down the stringent demands of the Faith so that they no longer shock or terrify. It has reduced the offence of the Cross to a doctrine. And it has separated the life of faith so effectively from the hard, brutal life of the world—either by its pietism or by its liberal humanism—that its pronouncements on the real questions of human living are no longer taken seriously, even by the majority of its own members.

2. *The Dissolution of the Parish*

Now it is a fact that in every country to-day, and among churchmen of every communion, there is tremendous concern being expressed at this divorce of the institutional Church from the ordinary life of men and women. Not only are we at last beginning to realize that the institutional Church is failing in its primary task. The path by which we are discovering our failure is also leading us to recognize that the Church has long since ceased to be anything but a pale reflection of the true Christian community. It is a point of experience to which an increasing number of ministers are coming. And I believe that on the Church's attitude to this problem depends, not only its future effectiveness, but its future existence as an institution.

What answers are, in fact, being given? There are those, of course, who refuse to recognize that the problem exists, and who believe that the institutional Church—subject as it has always been to periods of advance and recession—will safely ride out the storm. It is recorded somewhere' that during the days of the October *coup* in 1917, while the leaders of the Russian revolution were meeting in a house in a Moscow street, the leaders of the Orthodox Church were meeting in another house in the same street. And the religious leaders were discussing vestments. There will always be some blithe spirits who seem to be incapable of concern no matter what the signs of the times may be. There are others who are simply blind to these signs. It is part of our tragedy in the Church to-day that so many of us—ministers and people alike—contrive to maintain our cavalier optimism in spite of all that is going on around us. We enjoy the long picnic on the green grass, as P. T. Forsyth reminded us, while the floods are already gathering in the hills.

There are others who, seeing the collapse in the conventional pattern of the Church's life, demand the most radical revision of that pattern in the light of modern needs and changing demands. This seems to be the common attitude among the most forward-looking clergy and laity, not only in this country but abroad, and takes the form, negatively, of an attack on the traditional parochial system, and, positively, of the promotion of new ' communities ' based on common professional or cultural interests.

The Abbé Godin, that gifted and devoted man who

gave himself so unsparingly to the work of the Mission de Paris, believed that he could only establish communication with the lost proletariat by working outside the framework of the parish, and ' founding small Christian communities living in the milieu and radiating Christianity from their very midst '. This the existing parish could never do, and over it might be hung, Godin suggests, the placard of the legendary pianist in the American theatre : ' Do not shoot the pianist, he is doing his best.' The parish, effective possibly at another time and in another situation, is no longer able to make any significant contribution to the missionary task of the Church.

This same distrust of the traditional parochial system is responsible for a great deal of the most recent experiments in evangelism within the Protestant communions. The Protestant Professional Associations in France, the Evangelical Academies in Germany, the Zoë and Aktines Movements in Greece, Sigtuna in Sweden, the Christian Workers' League, and the new Christian Industrial Order in Scotland—all of these are an attempt to reach people at a point where there is a genuine community based, not on the place of residence, but on a common ground of interest.

Although it is by no means clear what relationship— if any—these functional groups are to bear to the established institutional Church, it appears, at least in France, that ultimately the functional groups will be brought together into a congregation, ' which will then become a community-of-communities '. In which case, one infers, the established Church will simply become redundant and conveniently disappear. Meanwhile, a minister in a city parish, who is deeply aware of the

inadequacy of the life and witness within his own
parish, presumably keeps the wheels of a dead system
turning until the new community-of-communities
emerges.

It is obvious that these movements are among the
most significant things that are happening in the Church
to-day. In so far as they are concerned with the training of laymen to make an effective witness to their
faith, and in so far as they are genuinely seeking to
penetrate the barriers which separate the secular world
from the message of the New Testament, they must be
given the undivided support and encouragement of the
Church. But can they provide any real alternative to
the traditional pattern of the Church's life out of the
ineffectiveness of which they have been born?

It would appear that they rest on a well-founded pre-
supposition. The disintegration of the family as the
stable unit of social life if not an accomplished fact in
this country as it is in France, for example, is nevertheless an imminent possibility. It is also true that a man's
primary experience of community to-day—especially
in urban areas—lies not in the district where he resides
but in the factory where he works and in the place
where he spends his leisure. But might it not be argued
that the shift of emphasis revealed in these new movements is indeed an escape from facing up to a more
radical issue, and an admission of defeat? Furthermore,
do they not merely push the problem a stage further
back? Whether these new groups are regarded as
' para-communities '—somewhere between the world
and the Church—or as valid Christian communities in
themselves, will the same problems which paralyse the
institutional Church not in time make their appearance

there—under a different guise, perhaps, but none the less real?

Again, it might be argued that these functional groups or cells cannot by their very nature be called ' Christian communities' in the deepest sense. Since they are formed on the basis of a common cultural or professional interest, it follows that they must of necessity be exclusive fellowships, drawing their members from one background, and in most cases from one social class. It is not denied for a moment that such cells for witness and action are of paramount importance in present-day evangelism, but how far does their inevitable exclusiveness square with the essential idea of the Christian community, one of the primary marks of which is its reconciling power, its inclusive character, its capacity to unite within itself men and women of every type and background? Apart altogether from the fact that these functional groups are rarely grounded in any act of sacramental worship.

It seems to me that there is in all this a dangerous tendency to idealize the secular community—the workers' world, for example—and almost to regard it as being in itself ' Christian ', simply because there is evidence of some kind of sense of community to be found there. The Abbé Godin was not infrequently accused by his fellow-priests of idolizing the proletariat and being incapable of finding any faults in it. And certainly one cannot read his book without being aware of at least a tendency in that direction. I have myself spoken to some ministers who are so profoundly conscious of the failure of the parochial system that they are prepared to go the length of saying that God has in fact ceased to speak through his Church, and that his Word is being heard to-day in the so-called pagan world. Such an attitude proceeds out of a double mis-understanding. It betrays a curious blindness to the true meaning of the Christian community; and it also betrays a profound misunderstanding of the nature and function of the Church itself. That the conventional pattern has failed is becoming almost an axiom. That the solution to the dilemma raised by its failure is to be found in the creation of functional groups, independent of the institutional Church is by no means axiomatic. There are those who believe the answer has to be found within the Church itself, and who realize all that this involves in conflict and heartbreak for those who seek such an answer.

It is easy to uncover the faults and failings of the traditional order of the Church's life. It is supremely tempting to cut oneself off from so much that contra-dicts the essence of the Faith, and dams up the channels of divine grace. But at the end of the day I am com-pelled to recognize that the failure of the Church is my own failure as a minister, and that the answer to it lies within myself. To realize that is our despair: it is also our hope.

3. *The Church within the Church*

Near the beginning of my ministry I had asked the question: How are my people to be brought to a sense of their missionary responsibility, so that we can estab-lish contact with those around us who are outside the sphere of the Church's influence?

At the end of my third year in North Kelvinside the question had been given at least a half-answer. The

Mission of Visitation not only brought us into contact with the people in the parish. It created within the congregation a new sense of mission. Apart from a tiny and non-vocal opposition, it was true to say that the congregation had become—at least so far as its own parish was concerned—missionary-minded.

But as time passed we became increasingly aware that we were failing to integrate those who had been won through the visitation into the full Christian experience. I have tried to analyse the cause of that failure. I have suggested that it lay essentially in the fact that we did not possess within ourselves the resources to meet the new demands that were being made on us. The conventional pattern of the Church's life had broken down. And there were times when I sincerely wished that we had never undertaken that door-to-door visitation. We had seen a great number of people being brought back to the church. But what had we to offer them? Had the parish nothing to give to them?

It was then that I began to see the need for the development of a new pattern of life within the congregation as a first priority. What is the point of evangelism if we are incapable of assimilating the converts? And where do we begin? Is it possible, in fact, for the parish to provide the answer to these questions? Can it become a 'living cell in the everlasting Church', exercising a redeeming influence on the whole community in which it is set?

As I cast about for an answer to these baffling questions in the third year of my ministry I saw that the situation within my own congregation had radically changed. Whereas at the beginning I had felt that I was working alone, now I saw that out of the Mission of

Visitation there had emerged a group of lay people, representing every section in the congregation, who had found in the Mission a new experience of the Faith. There were not many of them—perhaps twenty in all. A few were elders, some were Sunday school teachers, others members of the Women's Guild. Their horizon had been broadened. Their understanding of their faith had been deepened. Indeed for some of them the Mission had been the instrument of their conversion. These people were inarticulate and untrained. Neither they nor I had any idea how they might be used. But they were ready for service, and were clearly concerned to explore the deeper issues of membership in the Church. I began to realize the significance of that group and its emergence marked a new stage in the life of the parish.

And here I want to stress this point. The Church is gravely concerned with its evangelistic task. It is also concerned to ask how this obligation can be met. Generally we are told that there is no point in doing the work of evangelism until we are better prepared within our own churches. While this appears to be a self-evident truth, it involves in fact a peculiar paradox. The only way to prepare a church for evangelism is by the work of evangelism. Most of us realize that we have an imperative need to re-examine the pattern of our church's life, and find our way towards some more dynamic and relevant form of Christian community. We also realize the supreme urgency of finding some answer to the problem of communicating our gospel to the masses outside the Church. My own profound belief is that these two things are inextricably bound together, inter-related and inseparable. When we ask ourselves how to overcome the colossal barriers of ignorance and bewilderment which separate the mind of modern man from the message of the New Testament we can be sure that there is no adequate answer which does not at the same time recognize the need for a radical revision in the life and witness of the Christian community itself.

But there is no precedence in point of time. It is a mistake to say that we must cleanse the inner life of our church before we undertake the work of evangelism, and strengthen the faithful before we set about reclaiming the lapsed or challenging the careless. The faithful can only be strengthened in so far as they are going out to the lapsed and the careless. The inner life of the church can only gain reality in so far as the church is meeting its missionary responsibilities.

Such, at least, has been my own experience. The group which has proved to be the key to evangelism in my own parish emerged out of a mission for which they did not seem to have any equipment beyond a loyalty to their church. They went out on what was for them, of necessity, a simple mission of friendship. But it was there that they met Christ, and received a new commission. The story of my own work since that time is largely the story of the development of that group.

In his book, *The Idea of a Christian Society*, T. S. Eliot distinguishes between what he calls ' the Christian Community '—the institutional Church—and the ' Community of Christians '—which is the ' Church within the Church ', a group with no definite outline, consisting of both clergy and laity, and owning a common allegiance to Jesus Christ. A very similar idea underlies Emil Brunner's most recent book, *The Mis-understanding of the Church*. He draws a distinction between the *ecclesia*—which is the supernatural *koinonia* or fellowship of Jesus Christ—and the Church, the historical institution. This basic idea of a 'Church within the Church' gave us a working hypothesis which squared with our own immediate experience, and seemed to offer a line of concrete and specific action.

Is it not true that in every congregation there is a 'Church within the Church'? I remember D. P. Thomson putting it like this. The people in our churches, he said, correspond very closely to the people who surrounded Jesus during his earthly ministry. There were the five thousand—the curious, the interested crowd who came to see the miracles. And so in our churches there are the five thousand—the 'fringers', the occasional worshippers who appear mostly on Communion Sunday, but who remain on the periphery of the church's life. Then there were the seventy—the people whom Jesus sent out two by two. These people are represented in every congregation—they are the dependable workers, the leaders of the organizations, seldom articulate, but loyal to their church. Then there were the twelve—the small band of men who had been confronted by Christ, and who had responded to his call. A narrower circle in our congregations, perhaps, but present in most of them. Then, finally, there were the intimate friends of the Master who went with him to the Mount of Transfiguration—Peter, and James, and John. Are there not in our midst that tiny handful of those who have truly 'been with Jesus'?

Our task as ministers, D. P. Thomson suggested to me, is to bring the people from the fringe into the seventy;

to bring the seventy to a full and mature discipleship; and to ascend the Mount of Transfiguration with those who share Christ's intimate fellowship.

A fanciful picture? Not at all. I found within my own congregation that it was almost an exact reflection of the situation. Of course there are dangers in it— most particularly the dangers of Pharisaism and perfectionism. But in my own parish a group had emerged committed at a deeper level than anything I had previously known in the Church, and demanding some practical field of service in which to express their faith. It was a fair cross-section of the membership of the church, including as it did both old and young, both men and women. It possessed, even at that stage, a sense of fellowship or community very different from the inchoate sense of unity within the congregation itself. I began to feel that with this group lay the future of the work in North Kelvinside. Perhaps it might form the nucleus of a dynamic community capable not only of penetrating the secular world around us but also of assimilating those who were brought into the fellowship of the Church? Perhaps it held some answer to the powerlessness of the traditional parish system to cope with the new demands facing it? Perhaps—since it was completely identified with the institutional Church—it escaped the problems confronting those functional groups about which I have written? Perhaps out of this group might proceed a new pattern of parochial life?

During the next two years we were to discover the answer to these questions.

IV

THE PLACE OF THE LAYMAN

1. The Apostolate of the Laity

IT is generally accepted that the effective propagation of the Faith in the secular world depends ultimately on the witness of the layman. The idea of the apostolate of the laity is being eagerly examined by the Church in every country and in all denominations, and its far-reaching implications for the work of evangelism are beginning to be recognized even in those churches where the doctrine of the priesthood of all believers has not been central. In a pamphlet issued a year or two ago by the Scottish Churches Ecumenical Committee the necessity of lay witness is put as clearly as it could be: 'How is the Christian message to be presented to the secular world? Plainly the message must be brought to the world, for the world which nowadays will scarcely attend a political meeting is still less likely to attend a religious one. The message, then, must be delivered at the point where the Christian front meets and engages the world—i.e. at that part of the front which is occupied by the lay members of the Church witnessing to the Faith in their daily avocations.'

This concern for the apostolate of the laity has resulted in the emergence of a multitude of movements ranging from breakfast clubs for senators and congressmen in Washington, D.C., to the significant work of the Ecumenical Institute at Bossey, Switzerland. The Protestant Professional Associations in France, the Evangelical Academies in Germany, the Zoë-Aktines movement in Greece, the Church and World Institute in Holland—all these movements have a common object, the development of effective lay witness in the secular world.

For the parish minister, engaged in the hard and often unrewarding tasks of congregational and parochial work, it is at once stimulating and disheartening to read of these movements. He accepts implicitly the idea of the lay apostolate: but all too often he finds it impossible to translate the idea into practice in his own parish. The difficulties in the way are enormous, and in most writings on the subject these difficulties are either by-passed or disregarded.

At the outset, he is faced with the simple problem of finding laymen in his own congregation who have any real grasp of their responsibility for witness in the secular world. The laity have been called 'the unemployed of the Church', and there are several factors contributing to their state of unemployment. But the most important one is the 'clericalism' of the Church. Even in the Church of Scotland which, with its Presbyterian order, theoretically recognizes the place of the layman in the conduct of its affairs, the voice of the layman is seldom heard, and very little opportunity is afforded him to exercise any kind of 'non-pastoral' ministry. And the layman has not only come to accept this kind of clericalism as part of the natural ordering of the Church's life; he is also most reluctant to welcome a change. In his mind the minister's duties have become clear-cut and well defined, and the ordinary layman is content to leave it at that.

There is another difficulty which the parish minister finds at the local level. He may have about him a small group of people who realize their responsibility as Christians for active service in the work of the Church and positive witness in their daily avocations, but who feel that they do not possess the equipment to undertake it. Particularly in Scotland, where we are traditionally reticent in speaking about our own personal faith, and where such personal confession is regarded as exhibitionism, does this difficulty make itself felt.

These things have been brought home to me in the past few years in visiting scores of churches in different parts of the country seeking to enlist volunteers for local missions of visitation. Time and again I have found myself speaking to people who had literally never thought of such work as a possible field of service. Visitation is the minister's job, or, in certain circumstances, the elders'. And if, at the end of an evening of question and discussion and appeal, a handful of people might be prepared to admit that it was their responsibility, they hesitated at the thought of speaking to another person about the Faith.

In my own congregation these initial difficulties had been overcome. A group of lay people had emerged, representative of the whole congregation, and honestly committed to the work of evangelism within their own parish and to the business of ' witnessing to their faith in their daily avocations '. But it was precisely at this point that the real issues of the lay apostolate made themselves felt, both within the church, and more particularly within the experience of the layman himself.

It is hard enough to find laymen prepared to work out their salvation in terms of daily life. It is much harder to face the real implications of Christian witness, and offer the sincere layman guidance and direction and support in his attempt to take his religion out of the ghetto of the Church into the squalor and hostility of the market-place. Perhaps the professional Christians, the ministers and theologians, would be less glib in their advocacy of the lay apostolate if they had more practical experience of trying to live the Christian life in a single room in a slum tenement, or as a riveter's mate in a Clyde shipyard.

2. *To Be or to Act?*

One of the most penetrating studies of the layman's part that has recently appeared is in Jacques Ellul's book, *The Presence of the Kingdom*. M. Ellul is Professor of Law at Bordeaux University, and the manner of his own conversion to the Faith qualifies him to speak with authority on his theme—the communication of the gospel in a secular world, and the duties and demands which this world lays upon the Christian. He writes: ' In reality, to-day the theologian has nothing to say to the world, because there are no laymen in our churches; because, on the one hand there is the minister, who does not know the situation in the world, and on the other hand, there are " laymen ", who are very careful to keep their faith and their life in different compartments, or who try to escape from this dilemma by concentrating on ethics. Theological truth has no point of contact with the world . . . (and) God uses material means—in other words, He acts by His spirit through human instruments. Now it is this human instrument that our churches lack: that is why, when the gospel is preached, its message no longer reaches the world.'

M. Ellul goes on to examine the character of the situation which is to be addressed. He entertains no illusions about the modern world, regards it as 'the domain of Satan', and sees man dominated and controlled by facts—technics, the State, production. He then asks his question: What does it mean to be a Christian in this situation? And his answer to that question is of supreme importance for anyone who is concerned with the lay apostolate.

In a sentence he sums up his attitude: 'For Christians . . . what actually matters, in practice, is "to be" and not "to act".' With tremendous insight he deals with the modern obsession for action, particularly as it manifests itself in the Church, and exposes its inadequacy. Christian living is the first responsibility; and this 'being' takes the form of a threefold awareness: of the true meaning of our neighbour, 'the brother for whom Christ died'; of the Event, 'the intervention of one fact in the course of life, of history, of development . . . which includes within itself the meaning of all the development of the past, and significance for the future'; and of the frontier which exists between the profane and the sacred, the limit set to human pretensions by God. Given this awareness, a new style of life will emerge for the Christian, lived in tension between the secular world and theology, and creating a genuine point of contact for the communication of the gospel.

One last and immensely significant point M. Ellul

makes. He says that he will make no attempt to
describe this style of life, because at this juncture such
a description would remain purely intellectual, apart
altogether from the inherent danger of making the idea
a new law. But he emphasizes that any exploration of
the implications of this style of life must of necessity
be a corporate act. He writes: 'It is impossible for an
isolated Christian to follow this path. I believe, in fact,
that one of the essential conditions for its realization is
the substitution of a true solidarity among Christians
(a solidarity—voluntarily created by obedience to the
will of God) for the sociological solidarity, purely
mechanical in character, which is being dinned into
our ears, and which people want to make the basis of a
new world. In order to undertake this search for a new
"style of life", every Christian ought to feel and to
know that he is supported by others . . . further it
will evidently be necessary to engage in a work which
aims at rebuilding parish life, at discovering Christian
community, so that people may learn afresh what the
fruit of the Spirit is.'

I have dealt at some length with M. Ellul's book
because it throws fresh light on the whole problem of
the lay apostolate and the nature of Christian witness,
and because it offered me, as a parish minister trying
to understand the mind of those committed laymen
who were about me in my own congregation, a verifi-
cation of many things which I had arrived at tentatively
and experimentally in the course of my ministry.

3. The Point of Departure

For one thing, it is idle to speak of the lay apostolate to men and women who have no first-hand knowledge of the meaning of the Christian experience. So much of the Church's well-intentioned effort to enlist its laymen goes for nothing because it is concerned with action and organization, and not with what Ellul calls 'being'. In Scotland the most widespread attempts to work out the meaning of the lay apostolate have been undertaken at the level of Youth Fellowships, and in the past few years we have seen the development of a number of Christian 'action groups' among young people. Theoretically these action groups are necessary and inevitable if the idea of the lay apostolate is to be taken seriously. But so often—at least in my own experience—they have broken down after a year or two mainly because the demands of Christian action were being superimposed on young people who neither understood nor accepted the presuppositions on which Christian conduct is based. A vague and inarticulate identification with Christianity is not a sure enough foundation for building a Christian life. Something more is needed before we have any right to launch the layman into the tension of bearing a Christian witness in a hostile world. The precondition of Christian action is that 'being' of which Ellul has written, the conscious and personal appropriation of Christ which leads to a new 'style of life', and which in turn makes Christian action not only meaningful but possible.

In other words, before there is any hope of seeing the emergence of a genuine lay apostolate within our

Church we have to begin at the true point of departure. Action or witness which is not the spontaneous out-flow of a personal conviction and a personal encounter with Christ will soon run out and exhaust itself in mere humanitarianism.

There has been a profound reaction in our time against what is sometimes called ' Victorian evangelicalism ' or ' Conversionism '—and for very good reasons, which need not be gone into here. But one may take leave to wonder if the reaction has gone so far that we have thrown away in our modern Church the fundamental truth on which this so-called ' Conversionism ' rested—namely that Christianity is an intensely personal religion, and that a man cannot be a Christian by proxy. We have been so concerned to avoid the excesses and contradictions of evangelicalism that we have arrived at the paradoxical situation of eagerly seeking a lay apostolate within our churches and finding it hard to produce anything but a tiny handful of laymen who see any point in the apostolate. An example comes to mind from our own missionary work in Glasgow. At the turn of the century a considerable work was being done by the Presbytery in the lodging-houses of the city in the slum areas. Gradually through the years that work has been whittled down, not because it is any less urgent, but simply because the Church is incap-able of producing laymen to undertake it now that the original group of volunteers has died out. It is easy enough to find well-meaning people in our churches who will provide tea or organize a concert for the lodging-houses. But if anyone is needed to give a ten-minute address or lead in prayer we have to go to the mission halls or the Christian Brethren.

Of course we can rationalize our failure in this regard by pointing to the subjectivism of evangelical religion, or by pointing to the dichotomy between its profession and its practice. But most of us know that we are rationalizing, and that the lay apostolate will never be anything but a pious hope unless we are prepared to recognize that Christian action which does not emerge out of a personal faith is a contradiction in terms.

The second profoundly important principle to which Ellul's book pointed me was this—that the personal appropriation of the Christian 'style of life' has no meaning unless its implications are worked out as a corporate act.

There is an implicit tension in the Church of Scotland to-day which is variously described. It is interpreted by some as a tension between the old 'Free' Church tradition and the 'Parish' Church tradition, uneasily brought together in the Union of 1929—and that may very well be at the heart of it. In other words, it is a conflict between two doctrines of the Church. By others it is regarded as arising out of an unresolved tension in the approach to public worship, and the liturgical revival of the last thirty years has served to emphasize the tension. Or again, it is described as a conflict between the old evangelicalism and the new emphasis on community, with its demand for Christian social action and its 'Incarnational' theology. It has always seemed to me that this tension is unreal and indefensible, and that the true path of advance, at least as far as the Church of Scotland is concerned, lies in its resolution. I have tried to point out that there is a fundamental truth in evangelical religion which it is necessary to preserve. Equally I am convinced that its inevitable 'personalism' has to be guarded against. Too often the concern for individual salvation meant a complete indifference to the Church, and a retreat from the actual world in which men earn their bread. Henri Perrin, in his book, *Priest-Workman in Germany*, tells how he met thirty young Seminarians, eager, enthusiastic, dreaming of conquering the world. But he writes of them: 'Often, spirituality meant simply holding on to certain pious practices—"my" prayers, "my" interior life—and led to a tendency to cut themselves off, to be always on the defensive against their environment, to remain in their shell. You would have thought that they had nothing to offer the world dying beside them—as if they were beaten and flattened out by the life seething round them.' The evangelical Christian so often lives in this kind of vacuum, and fails to recognize the relevance of the Faith for his daily life.

Now when Ellul stresses the importance of the community as the indispensable factor in working out the Christian style of life it appears to me that he is going far towards bridging this wholly artificial gulf between personal faith and the demand for Christian social action. He is reminding us that Christian witness begins within the individual; but he is also reminding us that the idea of an isolated Christian is impossible, and that fundamentally a true lay apostolate presupposes the existence of a community in which and through which the Holy Spirit may speak.

In his book, *Return to Christianity*, Nels Ferré has expressed it succinctly: 'The deepest failure is not the failure of organization, but the failure of the Christian Church to be a vital Christian fellowship. Organiza-

tion is important for in an ideal organization the pat-
terns of reaction are conducive to co-operation.
Common interests and responsibilities tend to draw
people together. But organization is not enough. It
is not even primary . . . we must have indispensably
a new, sweeping Christian revival *which is bigger than
the old conversionism and deeper than the old social
gospelism*. The full vision and all-round responsibility
of the Christian faith must be preached in life and
power until it calls man to penitence before God and
to an all-transforming social responsibility. We may
have to start with prophetic individuals who can lead
because they know how to follow the true light. We
may have to have live cells of Christian community
springing up like oases within our parched churches.
These intensive groups of Christian fellowship will
prescribe for themselves ways of walking together that
spring out of a concern for people in all their troubles
and sorrows. Groups of concrete fellowship centred
around study, prayer, and work may give the vision and
power that can affect a Christian institution.' The
Church, Ferré reminds us, is the only *locus* of solution.

The whole idea of the apostolate of the laity is therefore explosive and revolutionary, and confronts us
with a threefold challenge.

First of all, it compels us to wrestle with the
supremely difficult task of leading men and women to a
point of decision in which the Faith becomes a personal
possession. This is by no means to say that the only
valid conversion is the sudden, emotional, ' time-and-
place' conversion associated with revival meetings,
although that may be the path along which many of
our best laymen will come. It is not important that a

man can say that in such a place and at such a time he
became a Christian. It is supremely important that any
man who is expected to bear a Christian witness should
know beyond any shadow of a peradventure where he
stands now. He should be a man for whom penitence
and faith are not merely theological terms, but an
expression of his own experience of God. No distinc-
tive Christian witness is possible without it.

The idea of the lay apostolate presents us with an
inescapable challenge, in the second place, because if
it is taken seriously it will mean upheaval and revolution within the conventional framework of the Church's
life. The group which emerges to seek a true Christian
solidarity, to be an oasis within our parched Church,
will find itself in inevitable conflict with those who are
content with things as they are, and who set their face
against any change in the ordered and traditional pattern. Such a group will not find an outlet for its
energies, a sphere in which to express itself, in the
routine of Mothers' Meetings, Men's Clubs and Dramatic
Clubs which go to make up the weekday activities of
any normal congregation. 'Only a revolution *within*
the churches,' writes Canon Collins, 'a revolution of
thought and outlook and of the whole " set-up " can
make them effective instruments in God's hands for the
evangelizing of this country : and only Christians who
are revolutionary in thought and outlook and their way
of life can hope to be effective evangelists to-day.'
Wherever a cell or group for lay witness comes into
being within a church it will involve tension and conflict. And that is the price we have to pay for taking
the lay apostolate seriously.

The third challenge of the lay apostolate is perhaps

the most difficult of all, and has already been hinted at in this chapter. When this group of people comes forward, drawn from different backgrounds and types, to explore the demands of Christian discipleship, it becomes immediately evident that new methods of instruction and training and new levels of Christian fellowship have to be explored if we are to keep faith with the layman. What happens, for example, when a business man with a family discovers that his business methods can no longer be squared with his new standard of judgment? What happens when a girl feels compelled to give up her job because she cannot obey the instructions of her employer and remain true to her faith? What *are* the determining factors for a man employed in a shipyard or a woman struggling to bring up a family in a one-room tenement house?

The lay apostolate may possess tremendous possibilities for the propagation of the Faith in a secular world. Let us also be assured that, if we allow it to become anything more than an idea in the mind of the professional theologians, it will lead us into unsuspected conflict. But for the Church, as for the individual, the point of conflict is the point of growth.

V

THE CONGREGATIONAL GROUP

1. Restoring the Community

I HAVE been trying to set down the stages through which my own ministry passed in these first few years, and to analyse those insights, if I can call them that, which determined the particular emphases which I came to regard as primary. There are no blue-prints for a parish ministry. Our teachers are—at the deepest level—the people among whom we are working. Our surest guides are very often those men and women who live outside the sphere of the Church's influence, and with whom our work brings us into contact only from time to time.

Gradually three principles became articulate for me, and I began to hold them with increasing conviction. The first is that the solution to the vast problem of communicating the gospel to the masses who live outside the sphere of Christian fellowship is inextricably bound up with the local church—that the key to evangelism lies in the parish. Secondly, that the Church can only fulfil its function, and penetrate the secular world when it is exhibiting the life of a genuine and dynamic Christian community—the *koinonia* of the New Testament. And thirdly, that in all this the place of the layman is decisive.

It was about this time that I came across a book

which has had a profound influence on my own thinking, and which I still regard as the most challenging
statement on the work of the parish ministry that I
have read. The book is the Abbé Michonneau's *Revolution in a City Parish*, and it should be made a text-book
for students in every divinity faculty in the country.
Granted that the situation in France is different in so
many ways from the situation in our own country,
Michonneau nevertheless emphasizes things that we
have forgotten, and by the overwhelming sincerity of
his own faith compels us to re-examine the whole pattern of our ministry.

He is completely convinced that the evangelization
of pagan France depends on the parish. He writes: ' If
. . . we strip off routine and turn boldly to new forms
of the apostolate, the parish becomes a living cell,
destined to propagate itself over an entire district. Then
we can see it has its rôle to play in this missionary
endeavour '. Unlike Godin, for example, he believes
that the parish cannot be by-passed, that it is strategically the key to the situation. ' Firstly, because it is
already existing. Whether it plays its rôle or not, *hic
et nunc*, the parish is a fact. It is, by right, if not in
reality, that tiny cell of Christianity, of the Incarnation.
. . . Every community has its own. Not even the civil
government is as well organized, for many a district
has several parishes. . . . And that is not all, for a
parish is equipped. It has its priests, and parish clergy
have always been the mainstay of the Church's force.
They live in the midst of those whom they are evangelizing. They are, or can be, or should be in permanent
contact with their people. . . .'

I do not think we can over-emphasize the importance

of this mere physical equipment which is at our disposal. And consider, as Michonneau does, the vast potential within our parishes of committed people—men and women living in the midst of the secular world, and capable, with the right direction, of exercising a tremendous influence upon it. He sums up: ' However forceful or generous or ingenious may be specialized methods, it will always be the parish which represents the main strength of the attack, like the infantry of an army. Like the infantry, it will be beaten if it fails to use new armaments and tactics, but it remains the indispensable means of holding any point of attack.'

Within my own congregation there began to emerge, after the first Mission of Visitation, a small and inarticulate group of people who were really concerned to explore at the deepest level the meaning of their membership in the Church. As time passed I began to realize that here in this group there was the nucleus of a dynamic community, a ' Church within a Church ', which bore at least some traces of that first *koinonia* which challenged the pagan world and planted the Cross at the heart of the Roman Empire.

Such a community must be an organic growth. It is obvious that it cannot be artificially created by a mere decision of the will. It is easy to form a club of people who happen to share a common interest in badminton, or dramatics, or country dancing. With a genuine community it is different. If it is to have any reality it must include within itself people of widely divergent interest and background and age-groups. The community cannot be established by decree. It must discover its own existence. And this is precisely what happened in my own church. These people in the group did not come together. They were driven together by their own failure to fulfil what they clearly saw to be their obligations as members of the Body of Christ. And their realization of failure was not gained through a mere theoretical speculation on the demands of Christ. It was discovered in the doing of his will.

As the congregational group began to discover its existence, so it began also to discover its function. First of all, the group exists as a training school in Christian discipleship. The members of the group had become painfully aware of their own inadequacy as they went round on door-to-door visitation, and as they tried to witness to their faith in their daily avocations. They saw that they had to learn, or learn again the rudiments of their own belief. They saw what little knowledge they had of the Bible—their text-book. They were driven to re-examine the attitude of the New Testament to the crucial problems which arose for them every day in their business. And so, in the congregational group, we began to study together the fundamental facts of the Faith, the relevance of the Christian ethic to the demands of the world in which we earn our bread; and to share, in common discussion, those baffling problems which confront any man who is seriously trying to be true to the mind of Christ.

The group has a second function which can only be described as ' an attempt to restore the parochial community '. We are all familiar with the dreadful anonymity which exists in any city parish. I have tried to show how, in my own parish, I did not find a community, but a broken, divided, inchoate mass of people. And in this situation our congregations are as often as not mere aggregates of individuals who have little more than a nodding acquaintance with one another. If we believe that the parish—or the congregation—should be what one writer has called 'the local and universal seat of the redemption'; if we believe that the Christian community should in some way be a constant 'representation of the Incarnation', then it is clear that our traditional set-up is inadequate and badly in need of overhaul. In the Amsterdam report, *The Church's Witness to God's Design*, there is this significant paragraph: 'Even in so-called Christian countries, the actual state of the parish in all towns and in many rural areas is that it consists of a small nucleus of churchgoers, and a very much larger mass of occasional conformists, the indifferent and the hostile. The natural activity of the Christian ought to be, and usually is not, that which is described by the expressive French word *rayonnement*. In the parish setting evangelism is not a matter of occasional special efforts, but a permanent element in all church activities, and that for which the whole worshipping community recognizes that it is being trained. The evangelizing agent is not the ordained minister, but the whole Christian fellowship.' The congregational group exists, then, to translate this idea of *rayonnement* into a practical reality.

Which leads to the third function of the group—the outcome of the first two. It exists as an evangelizing agency—or more correctly, it provides an outlet in which its members can find the opportunity to express their faith in terms of service. It is committed to both direct and indirect evangelism, with three specific fields of operation. First of all, it works within the congregation of which it is a part. Its members—by their own witness and example—are seeking to bring others into the sphere of the group's life and work. It acts, secondly, within the community around it, through direct evangelistic activity in house-to-house visitation, open-air meetings and missions; and through the indirect evangelism of practical service. The members of the group, in other words, may be prepared to give a reason for the faith that is in them at a street-corner or in a public meeting. But they are also prepared to scrub out the kitchen of an invalid mother or accept responsibility for a destitute family. And finally, the members of the group are committed to the task of making a decisive Christian witness in their places of work and business and leisure. This may mean active involvement in the Trade Union movement. It may lead to the formation of a Christian cell in an engineering shop. It may demand the sacrifice of security to maintain Christian standards in the conduct of business.

The members of the group are under no delusions about the enormity of the undertaking to which they have committed themselves. They are not plaster saints. They are a handful of very frightened people, very often tempted to go back to the comfortable conformity from which most of them have come, frequently prone to failure and stumbling in their attempts to make articulate the convictions which they hold. More than once since our first coming together we have drifted close to dissolution. The group has shattered our complacency and confronted us with demands which we would fain avoid. And yet we know that there is no turning back. Some of us have tried it, and we have found—miraculously—that the Christ who has called us to this work will not leave us alone. If we have discovered the agony of seeking to follow Christ, we have also discovered the depths of his grace.   Always he is waiting for us on the road, sending us back to bear the cross of discipleship.

I would like to be able to report that the congregational group has been a tremendous success.   It has not. It has raised at least as many problems as it has solved. But we believe that they are the problems not of decay, but of growth.

2. The Group in Action

In his book, *Signs of Hope in a Century of Despair*, Elton Trueblood speaks of the growth of redemptive societies, and writes: 'The essence of the new development is the discovery or rediscovery of the explosive power that lies in a really committed group who seek to witness *together* to the life and reality of the Living Christ.'   The principle is at least theoretically accepted in every communion of the Church.   In the Anglican booklet, *Towards the Conversion of England*, this recommendation is made: 'That in every congregation there should be formed groups or cells of people who have the concern for evangelism deeply at heart, and are prepared to give time and effort to it . . . and that these groups should be composed of those who desire, by habits of personal devotion, by study, by planning together, by pooling experience, to equip themselves for ordinary, everyday witness to Christ in their neighbourhood, at their work, and in their leisure.'   The idea is at least theoretically accepted.   It is a different matter, however, to translate the theory into practice, and guide the development of such a group within one's own parish.   That there is an explosive power in such a committed group there can be no doubt at all. But it is a power which not only solves problems—it creates them. perhaps that is why there is so much talk about the apostolate of the laity and so little action. It was Dostoievsky who said that love in action is much more terrible than love in dreams.

The group began to emerge after the first campaign of visitation in 1947. It took on an articulate shape during the Glasgow Churches Campaign of 1950. Over a period of a week I conducted a ' mission to the congregation ', in which I spoke exclusively to those people in my own church who are interested enough to appear at a week-night meeting of a purely religious nature. I gave a course of addresses on the nature and function of the Church and the responsibilities of membership; and on the following Sunday, after the evening service, those who desired to make a more positive commitment of heart and life to the Lord Jesus Christ and the service of his Church than they had done before were asked to remain for a brief service of rededication. This service of rededication was held after the normal diet of worship so that no one would feel obliged to stay or be embarrassed because he did not come forward. To that service just over a hundred people came—about a tenth of the membership. They renewed the vows they had taken when they first came into full membership in the Church and pledged themselves to study together the full implications of these vows. A few months afterwards this group took part in a large-scale visitation of the whole community with the other churches in the district as part of the Glasgow Campaign, and when that was finished they began to meet as the congregational group.

During the first winter we met weekly, with an average attendance of fifty. We undertook a planned course of New Testament studies for the first part of the evening, then spent an hour in discussion and in what the Anglican booklet calls ' the pooling of experience ', and closed with a simple act of worship.

The membership of the group is representative of the whole congregation. It is an inclusive fellowship, drawing together into its membership old and young, men and women, employers and employees—housewives, teachers, factory workers, nurses, office-workers, university students and so on. It is an open fellowship. There are no conditions of membership. The meetings of the group are announced weekly from the pulpit, and anyone who is interested in what we are trying to do is free to come.

Perhaps the most striking thing that happened during the first winter was our simple discovery of the meaning of Christian community. The members of the group had for the most part known each other for years. They had worshipped in the same church week by week. They had attended the same organizations. But of Christian fellowship at the deepest level they had no experience at all. They had been caught up in the grim anonymity of a city church. It was an astonishing and heart-warming thing to see men and women who had been strangers to one another being drawn into a close fellowship in which the barriers were down. And this was no mere human fellowship. From the group itself came a request for more frequent celebration of the Sacrament of the Lord's Supper. Formerly we observed a quarterly Communion in our congregation. The members of the group, following a discussion one night on the sacraments, began to realize that Holy Communion itself is the very centre of the Christian community, and for the past year we have been meeting for a monthly Communion service in the church. This service is not, of course, confined to members of the group. And it has been startling to see how deeply appreciated the monthly Communion has been by the whole Church.

One other development of the first winter has determined the present shape of the group. We came to realize that the group was too large to fulfil its true purpose. And the realization came to us in the most painful way. For a long time we had been trying to help a young man—let's call him Alastair. Alastair is a child of his times. Coming to adolescence at the beginning of the war he got mixed up with the wrong sort of company and found himself in a remand home. From the time he was fourteen until we met him twelve years later he had never been out of prison for a period longer than six months. He was what the authorities would regard as an incorrigible. He appeared among us one night—brought by another man he had known in prison. It was plain to see that he was sick physically and spiritually. For months we did what we could for him. And then, for a spell, he disappeared. At a group meeting I asked if anyone knew what had become of Alastair. No one did. He was our responsibility, and we had failed. It was evident that the group was too big to maintain the kind of personal concern which we wanted to achieve. It was clear that we had to think again about the shape of our meetings.

We had very little in the way of precedents to guide us. But we decided to split the group into five cells, and hold the meetings in five different houses in the parish, under lay leadership. And so for three Wednesdays in the month the group meets like that, and comes together on the fourth week for common discussion and fellowship. There is no doubt at all that these house meetings have been far and away the most important thing that has happened.

For one thing, they have acted as a bridge between the parish and the group. It is much easier to invite an interested friend to a house than to a church meeting, and since the house meetings began the group has exactly doubled in size. Further, the smaller cells with their more intimate character have helped to make articulate people who found it hard to speak in a larger meeting. The five cells study the same passages of Scripture week by week, and share in the main meeting at the end of the month the questions and difficulties which have been raised. Each meeting ends with a brief act of worship conducted by the members in turn.

Through these house meetings we have begun to see the principle of *rayonnement* in action. They are centres of light for the whole parish, and their influence is felt further than we at first realized. It seems to me that they are pointing us to the rediscovery of a supremely important fact in the history of the Church —to what the Apostle called 'The Church in your home'. Was it not after this fashion that the Church had its first existence? And have we not lost something of infinite value in identifying the worship of God and the coming together of the Christian community almost exclusively with a building set apart for this specific purpose? When I think, for example, of the great new housing areas of our cities where it is impossible to provide adequate buildings for worship until years have elapsed and the community has been established, I believe that the situation provides a great opportunity for more daring experiments in new forms of Christian community which are independent of buildings.

In my own church we are continually lamenting the lack of hall accommodation. We have one small hall seating about a hundred and fifty people in which to accommodate all the multifarious activities which go to make up the ordinary life of a congregation. But could it be that the wisdom of those who first built the church has escaped us? Could it be that the secularism of the Church is the inevitable outcome of our failure to see that the Christian community exists not in 'activities' but in worship. And that in our own parish there is not one church, but hundreds? Or, at least, there is a church wherever two or three are gathered together in the name of Christ, the King and Head of the Church.

Along these lines we are seeking to fulfil the three-fold function which I have already outlined. The period of instruction has demanded a close study of the fundamental facts of our faith—the vows of membership which most of us once accepted without much thought. Dorothy Sayers has said somewhere that the average church member is 'about as well equipped to do battle on fundamentals with a Marxian atheist or a Wellsian agnostic as a boy with a pea-shooter facing a fanfare of machine guns'. And it was not long before the members of the group discovered how true the observation is. They realized their need for study and instruction, and in the group they are compelled to examine seriously the presuppositions which most of them had taken for granted. Through their common study and prayer, and through the work they are doing together we are beginning to see the restoration of a genuine parochial community, in which differences of background and training are being transcended, and which is making real both to the group members themselves and the people around the power of the Christian fellowship. And finally, they are finding new avenues of service, without which the Christian life withers and dies. We have discovered that the Church—when it is really alive—has more things to offer by way of practical work than singing in the choir or teaching a Sunday school class. The problem for those who take their faith seriously is not where to find a piece of work to undertake. It is rather to find time to carry out a fraction of what is laid upon them.

3. *The Overwhelming Minority*

Those who have read thus far will no doubt have observed that what began as the story of a Glasgow city parish is ending as the story of a minority group within the parish. That is wholly intentional. It is our conviction that the emergence of the congregational group has been the most significant thing that happened to us; and that this group in fact points the way forward towards a new pattern in parochial life which will supply at least some answer to the problem of bringing the message of the gospel to bear on the lives of those masses round our doors who regard the Church as a harmless irrelevance.

Most ministers live under the tyranny of numbers. The success or failure of a church is gauged not by the force of its spiritual impact on a community but by the number of members on its roll, or the size of its services, or the state of its finances. And, paradoxically, so long as we allow these things to tyrannize us it is most unlikely that we will ever placate the tyranny. My own experience has been that when we begin to see the power latent in that inner group of committed men and women who exist in all our congregations, and direct our energies towards the task of making that group a disciplined and trained spearhead for evangelism within the community, then we may begin to see the positive results for which most of us long.

We realize, of course, that this will involve a reassessment of our priorities as ministers. I remember once speaking to a certain congregation about the group in my own church. It was one of those congregations in which there exists a continual and unremitting whirl of activity, with clubs of all descriptions jostling for accommodation in the church buildings. On the face of it, it looked like a successful church. But when I spoke of a weekly meeting for Bible study and of small groups meeting for prayer, one office-bearer pointed out that in their church there was no time for this kind of thing, and that in any case members of the church should be too busy helping to run the organizations to find time for it. He also suggested in all seriousness that perhaps I could find better ways of occupying my time as a minister.

I reckon that this is not so far from the experience of most of us. We are so caught up in the conventional pattern of the Church's life, so busy keeping the wheels turning that we find it almost impossible to experiment with new forms of life within the Church. And any decision to go forward in this direction demands not only an act of faith but an act of courage in the face of inevitable opposition from members and office-bearers within our churches who are perfectly content with things as they are, and cannot for the life of them understand why they should be changed.

If there is, however, something of importance in this development of what have been called 'redemptive societies' within our congregations, we have still to ask how far this approach is likely to succeed against the conventional background of the Church's life. I am not at all certain about the answer to that question. The creation of any such group within a congregation or parish is bound to bring with it immense difficulties.

For one thing, the group can so easily become separatist, exclusive, and Pharisaical. It is interesting and significant to note that in my own group, in a church with an eldership of just over thirty members, only about a third of the elders regularly attended the meetings of the group. Furthermore, the people who do compose the group's membership are by no means most active in the organization and administration of the church's institutional life. These facts speak for themselves. And the existence of such a group in any congregation not only tends to drive the members of it into an inevitable 'holier-than-thou' attitude, but introduces an element of conflict and unease in the minds of those outside the group, which, far from bringing them in, only serves to drive them further away. This is obviously the most serious problem we have to face. It may vitiate the group's work in its first evangelistic responsibility—within its own congregation. And it compels us to ask how far such a group is practicable or legitimate within the framework of the conventional pattern of the Church's life, as it presently exists.

The second main disadvantage comes from within the group itself—I mean, the mixed character of its membership. No matter what precautions are taken to ensure the good faith, the sincerity, and the Christian awareness of the members, this kind of meeting inevitably attracts the crank, and the man with the one-track mind—usually a well-meaning and sincere fundamentalist, who can hold up the entire proceedings on some irrelevant point of Biblical interpretation.

A more serious danger is the danger of subjectivism and introspection. Again, in a meeting of this kind there is a tendency for the members to become intensely preoccupied with their own spiritual experience, to cut themselves off from the world around them. So that, instead of being fitted for active service, their instruction becomes a kind of narcotic against involvement.

Perhaps the most insuperable difficulty with such a group lies in the fact that tremendous differences exist between the members, not only in cultural background and experience, but—far more important—in spiritual capacity and awareness. While we recognize that there are no barriers at the Communion Table, we do not always live at the level of the Sacrament.

Yet we are quite sure in my own Church that the question remains. If the lay apostolate finds expression through the growth of these 'redemptive societies' within the Church; and if such groups have a real contribution to make both for the strengthening of the faithful and the recovering of the lapsed, how far can they—or should they—exist within the conventional framework of the Church's life?

There is no glib answer to the question. Yet we have become increasingly certain in our own parish that, in spite of the difficulties involved, we have to go ahead. We have no sensational results to record. But gradually we are beginning to see a new situation emerging in the parish. Lives are being changed. The sick are being healed through the prayers of the group. And the gulf between the parish and its church is being bridged. It has meant tension and conflict and mis-understanding. It has also served to remind us that the way of Christian discipleship is still the way of a Cross.

4. The Church—Collective or Community?

Dr. Emil Brunner ends his book, *The Misunderstanding of the Church*, with these words : ' During the whole course of its history, by reason of the fact that it was essentially a collective rather than a fellowship, the Church has not only neglected to create a true brother-hood in Christ, but in many ways has positively hindered such a development. Yet just here lies the essence of the New Testament *ecclesia*—the oneness of Communion with Christ by faith and brotherhood in love. Therefore efforts to create new forms of Christian communion at the present time are directed to this end and will be so much more in the future. It is because the Church has neglected in almost all ages to create a true fellowship in Christ that we are confronted by the phenomenon of modern communism which has grown like a wasting disease. *With or without the churches, if necessary even in opposition to them, God will cause the ecclesia to become a real community of brothers.* Whether the Churches yield to this recognition or on the contrary blind themselves to it will determine the question whether or not they have a future.'

Since I read these words I have kept wondering what people in Britain or America make of them. Here is one of the most eminent living theologians, a man closely in touch with modern trends, setting it down as a sober and mature opinion that the development of circumstances may spell the destruction of the institutional Church as we know it. And Dr. Brunner is by no means alone in his opinion. His view is increasingly shared by European and Eastern churchmen. Can it be that these men, living closer to the vast eruptions of our time, have allowed their judgment to become twisted, and are giving way to pessimism and despair? Or is it perhaps nearer the mark to suggest that their personal experience of the malignity of the decay in the modern world has led them to a prophetic insight denied to churchmen in Britain and America, for whom the pressures of our time remain theoretical and speculative?

It is a plain fact that the most daring and adventurous experiments in Christian community are coming from those countries where the full implications of the breakdown of Christian culture are clear-cut and unavoidable. In Britain and America, where we still retain the traces at least of a Christian culture, we are still thinking in categories which served the situation of another generation. We seem to be incapable of realizing that there is no Iron Curtain in the realm of ideas, and that the acids which have bitten so deeply into the life of Europe and Asia have already begun the process of corrosion in our own land.

It may be that we still have time to prepare to meet

the full power of the attack. But that will demand from our churchmen—ministers and people alike—a much deeper awareness of the kind of world we are living in, a more courageous attempt to cut a new way through the tangled dark undergrowth of our conventional church life, and above all a new experience of the Cross. Because it is there that our pride has to be broken and our complacency shattered. It is there that we enter fully into the meaning of human sin and the amazing, recreating grace of God. It is there that the true fellowship of Christ comes into being. With this redeemed community, which God is calling into existence, rests his work. It is not identifiable with the institutional Church and cannot ultimately be contained by it. If the Church remains a collective it will wither away. If, by the grace of God, we begin to bear the agony of seeing the Community of Christ coming alive, then God will use us for his own purposes.

VI

PLANNING A PARISH
MISSION

•

1. General Principles

IN this chapter I want to give some practical guidance
to ministers and laymen who are genuinely concerned
with the missionary task of the Church and who are
prepared to experiment with new methods of tackling
the missionary problem and new forms of life within
their own congregations.

I hasten to say that what follows is not to be regarded
as a blue-print for mission which, if followed to the
letter, will inevitably result in spectacular success.
There is no blue-print for evangelism. There are only
certain broad principles of approach which have to be
acted upon experimentally, and with a clear understanding that details of method and technique have to
be modified and adapted according to the peculiar
characteristics and demands of the local situation. It is
important to recognize, however, that these 'general
principles of mission' are increasingly being accepted as
valid for the whole Church, whether it is located in the
slums of Glasgow or London, or in one of the vast new
housing areas, or in an isolated rural community.

At the outset, therefore, we should remind ourselves
of these general principles upon which modern mission
has to be based.

The first principle, or point of departure, in our missionary planning must be the realization that the key to evangelism for the Church to-day lies with the parish or local congregation. I am not thinking of the parish at this point as a geographical or territorial entity, but as the community of Christians at worship and work and witness in the secular world. The task of the Church is to ' make the Confession heard in the sphere of the world ', and that can only be done when the Confession has been actualized in the life of the Christian community.

Arising from that is the second principle of mission, namely, that true and effective mission is not an occasional or sporadic effort but a continuous and coherent pattern of life within the Church. I might have called this chapter ' Planning a Missionary Parish ' rather than ' Planning a Parish Mission ', because it is my profound conviction that part at least of the ineffectiveness of our evangelism is due to our regarding it as a ' special activity to be undertaken at certain times, and not as the constant and spontaneous and inevitable outflow of our Christian experience. It is with the emergence of the missionary parish that the future of evangelism lies. When a congregation embarks, therefore, on a specific mission it should have two objectives in view. Its first objective is naturally to win the unchurched and to challenge the careless. But its second objective should be to quicken the life of the congregation itself, and lay the foundations of a missionary community. These things will be examined further when we look at the results of the parish mission.

The third general principle of mission which must underlie all our planning is that, whatever method of mission we adopt, the layman has a vital and strategic part to play. ' If the seventeen thousand priests of the Church of England,' said the writers of the Anglican report on evangelism, ' are to become seventeen thousand evangelists and trainers of evangelists, something far more revolutionary is demanded than the strengthening of auxiliary ministries open to faithful churchmen and churchwomen—nothing less, indeed, than the full co-operation of the whole body of the laity in the apostolate of the Church.'

These fundamental assumptions of modern mission, so widely accepted by the Church, are increasingly influencing the actual type of mission which forward-looking churches are undertaking. The ' Religion and Life Week ' type of campaign, with a visiting preacher conducting a series of evangelistic services, while it may have some contribution to make, is clearly seen to be inadequate. Its appeal is limited largely to the churchgoer—and to the faithful churchgoer at that; and it offers no scope for the layman. The type of mission which expresses those principles I have outlined is a mission centred on house-to-house visitation in a parish or district, and using all the resources at a church's disposal. It is with the practical planning of such a mission that the rest of this chapter is concerned.

2. *The Parish Mission*

The mission should be regarded as consisting of three parts, all of which are of equal importance, and all of which are indispensable. First, there is the period of preparation; second, there is the period of attack; and finally there is the period of follow-up. An effective parish mission is not something which can be carried out in a week or a month. If it is to be properly done —and this is true for every type of area—and if the three stages of preparation, attack and follow-up are to be given serious attention, then the mission will extend over a period of eighteen months or two years. Only such a long-term venture will yield the true fruits of evangelism. Mission is no tip-and-run affair—which, incidentally, is the most glaring inadequacy of the so-called ' Commando ' campaign. The commando unit in military strategy makes an important contribution to the whole operation; but its main purpose is to soften-up the ground, or gather information about enemy dispositions, or effect a diversion. And the ' Christian Commando Campaign ' can only be a tiny fragment in the whole pattern of mission. Unfortunately, it is frequently no more than a diversion—and not in the military sense.

The parish mission, then, should be planned to cover a period of eighteen months or two years. And let us be quite clear in our own minds before we embark upon it that if it is going to make demands upon us—both minister and people—far heavier than we can antici-pate, it will also lead us into a new and thrilling experience of Christian discipleship.

(i) The Period of Preparation

I have said earlier in this book that the best method of preparing a congregation for mission is the work of mission itself, and that indeed we cannot wait until the Church is prepared before we go out on the business of the Kingdom. My own congregation became alive to its responsibilities through the impact made by a visiting team of young people from outside the parish, and by the tentative efforts of a small handful of members to follow up the work that had been done. This still seems to me to be the best method of preparation. It is the method employed, for example, by the Rev. D. P. Thomson in his evangelistic work in Scotland. I have heard it called 'the chain-reaction' method. Mr. Thomson undertakes to lead a mission in a widespread area like the West Fife coalfields. He begins by taking to West Fife a group of lay people from an area in which he has previously conducted a campaign; and, by organizing a training school in one of the main centres of population and carrying out at the same time a house-to-house visitation with his trained workers as the spearhead, he enlists the interest and support of the local congregations. As the campaign progresses through the wide area volunteers from the town in which the work began travel to help the local churches in the new field. The testimony of these lay volunteers is far more eloquent and wins far more support from a congregation than any ministerial appeal. The layman who naturally regards the task of house-to-house visitation with trepidation or scepticism is more likely to be challenged and shaken out of his hesitation by the witness of a miner, who has travelled twenty miles after a shift at the coal-face to help in a parish which is not his own, than by any pulpit appeal for volunteers. In this way, preparation and mission go hand-in-hand. And wherever a congregation has carried out this type of campaign they might well consider offering to help a neighbouring parish by undertaking for it a preliminary visitation.

It is not often possible, however, for this kind of

initial impetus to be given; and, even when it is, there are practical steps in preparation to be undertaken. In this chapter I am thinking primarily of the minister who has gathered about him a small group of lay people, who is not in the way of receiving outside assistance, and who wants to know quite simply where to begin.

He begins, obviously, with his own congregation, and at the simplest level. Something has to be done to interest the whole membership in the mission, to outline the general plan, and above all to foster a sense of communal responsibility for it. Many congregations have found that this can best be done by organizing a series of social gatherings for the members during the first part of the winter session. These gatherings should be informal and friendly. They should not be so big as to become impersonal. In one church, with a membership of just under eleven hundred, the congregation was divided into six groups, and such a gathering was organized weekly over a period of six weeks in October and November. A personal invitation was posted to every member. The response was unexpectedly high— eighty-five per cent of the congregation attended. Not only was an excellent opportunity afforded for acquainting the people with the plan of campaign. These socials brought the whole congregation together at a level of simple friendship which they had not known before, and in the by-going we saw, in the weeks following, the return to the Sunday services of not a few lapsed and indifferent members.

This leads to the second stage of preparation at a deeper level—namely, to a mission in the congregation. In the spring of the year, preferably when the organizations have closed their normal activities, a week should be set apart for a series of meetings designed primarily for instruction. The people who can come to these meetings will be, on the whole, the people from whom we will draw the volunteers for visitation. We should aim at leading them to a more mature understanding of the nature and vocation of the Church, of the meaning of worship, and of the responsibilities of membership. Here an appeal should be made for volunteers who are prepared to go out to the parish, and at the end of the week a service of dedication should be held for those who come forward. In the vast majority of congregations where I have seen this type of approach carried out the minister finds that about a tenth of his membership have offered their services. With this nucleus of committed people, drawn from every section of his congregation, rests the real work of mission.

The third stage of preparation consists in the training of the volunteers. Many ministers and evangelists experienced in this type of house-to-house mission assert that the visitors should be hand-picked in order to avoid the embarrassment of getting the wrong kind of volunteer. My own view is exactly the opposite. Except that I normally make a lower age limit of seventeen, I make no other conditions. Time and again I have discovered that the person whom I would never have chosen for this work makes the most effective visitor. And in any case this work is primarily a witness by the Christian community; and that community is never selective.

A series of training classes should be held for the volunteers following the mission in the congregation, with ample opportunity for questions and discussion. The best speakers at such classes are invariably laymen and laywomen who have some experience of this work. Let them speak naturally of their own experience: and above all, let them speak honestly of it. This work is never easy for the layman to take upon himself. He is usually deeply conscious of his own inadequacy. He is anxious about the kind of questions he is likely to be asked in non-churchgoing homes. When we have done all that we can to prepare him for the work, we have still to tell him that he will learn more in his first night of actual visitation than he will learn from a score of lectures.

The group, then, is ready to go out. The period of preparation leads to the period of attack, and the task of house-to-house visitation begins. A group which has gone thus far is on the edge of a new kind of service with implications beyond anything they can imagine.

(ii) The Period of Attack

I have already written something of the actual work of house-to-house visitation earlier in this book, and all I want to do at this stage is to suggest one or two points for practical guidance.

First of all, *survey the area*. Before the visitation begins the area to be visited should be carefully defined, a map prepared for the guidance of the visitors, and a list made of the homes to be called upon. This list can be compiled from the electoral roll, and this preliminary work is well worth carrying out. It lets the group know the exact extent of its commitment. It allows those who are planning the mission to assess the time it will take to cover the area. And the visitors can go out knowing at least the names of the people they will visit. In addition this clerical work offers a field of service for many people who could not—or would not —volunteer for the visitation itself.

Second, *define the objective*. It seems to me that there are three levels at which this type of mission can be done, depending on the stage of spiritual maturity at which the group has arrived. They are not, of course, mutually exclusive, and may, in fact, all be characteristics of a single mission. First of all, it may be a simple mission of friendship, in which the members of a church go out to carry a greeting to every home in the parish or community, irrespective of church connection, and to extend an invitation to those with no church affiliation to attend the services and activities of the local church. Most congregations will begin at this level in their first parish mission.

The second type of house-to-house mission which may be planned more properly deserves the name of ' visitation evangelism ', as it has become known and practised in the United States. From my reading of the extensive literature on the work in that country, I gather that the primary objective of parish mission there is to afford trained lay workers an opportunity to do what used to be called ' personal work ' in the homes of the people upon whom they call—to ' win men for Christ '. I am making no judgment on this kind of mission. I am completely convinced that personal work of this nature must be a feature of any mission which is to be ultimately effective. Its danger lies in its individualism, in its exclusive emphasis on personal decision, and its tendency to fail to recognize the responsibility for a total witness in the secular world.

Which brings us to the third type of parish mission—

one which includes the other two but goes beyond them. It will be fundamentally a mission of service, a spontaneous outgoing of the Christian community. It will involve personal work—the leading of men and women into a decisive experience of Christ. But—and I realize the difficulty of writing this, and its liability to be misunderstood—these things will not be its primary objective. That will be service to a community for which Christ died, and to men and women who are our brothers and sisters because Christ died for them, service to them whether they accept Christ or not. In this kind of mission the volunteers have to be prepared to undertake a long and arduous task which will involve them in heartbreak and disappointment, and compel them literally to get their hands dirty in the business of the parish. At this point, however, we will assume that it is to be a mission of friendship—which is a necessary first step in the emergence of a missionary parish.

Having surveyed the area, and defined the immediate objective, the third practical step is to *prepare your literature*. It is an immense help to the hesitant and often inarticulate visitor to have something to carry in his hand which will offer a starting-point of conversation. The literature may be a simple leaflet bearing a message to the parish from the minister and office-bearers. Or the visitors may carry a selection of the Church's literature for sale to the contacts they make. My own feeling is that to sell literature on this kind of mission is not desirable, although in point of fact such an experienced evangelist as D. P. Thomson unhesitatingly recommends it. It should also be noted that door-to-door colportage has been largely left in the hands of sects like Jehovah's Witnesses, and in this a great field of missionary enterprise is unexplored by the Church. Again there must be adaptation to meet local circumstances.

The group or team is now ready to go out. This part of the mission should, in the first instance, be planned to cover a brief and concentrated period. With a team of a hundred volunteers, two thousand homes can be visited in ten weekdays. The team should meet for an evening meal and prayers together before they go out. It should be left open whether they go singly or in pairs. When they complete their allocation of visits they return to the church where a clerical staff is waiting to receive their reports, and tabulate the statistics. Supper and family worship, to which contacts made during the visitation can be invited, should close the evening's work.

These are only suggestions for guidance. Each local congregation will evolve its own method. There is nothing stereotyped about the form of a mission of friendship. Indeed—as in all mission—the greatest danger is probably the danger of over-organization which is liable to swamp the primary intention.

At the close of this 'period of attack', then, the minister and office-bearers should have a clear picture of their parish. They know the religious situation in their community—the homes connected with a place of worship and those with no connection. Valuable contacts have been established. Much useful information has been gathered. The work of follow-up is ready to begin.

Before we look at that, there is a point of real importance which might well be taken up at this stage. It is very often suggested that, while this type of mission may be effective in a city or town parish, it cannot be undertaken in a village or rural community. The argument is that in such a community the residents are so well known to one another that it would be inadvisable to ask any group of church people to carry out such a visitation if, indeed, they could be induced to volunteer for it. House-to-house visitation, it is argued, depends very largely on the anonymity of the city or town. The more intimate and conservative life of a country village or rural community makes it impossible.

The objection is certainly a serious one. I have seen this whole approach to mission rejected because of it. And yet, on the other hand, I have seen it most effectively undertaken where there is strong ministerial leadership and a proper appreciation of the difficulties involved. A visitation campaign is not impossible in a country parish. It is certainly more difficult, for the simple reason that it is infinitely harder to make a personal witness for Christ and his Church among people who know us intimately. But does this not, in fact, confront us with a challenge which cannot be avoided? Does it not demand a new level of personal consecration from our church members and office-bearers in country districts which compels them to evangelize in spite of the difficulties involved? Does it not suggest that the need for a positive and mature lay apostolate is even more apparent in the rural community than in the industrial centre? It is easy to make all kinds of rationalizations about the problem of mission in rural areas, to plead for a special approach to meet the peculiar conditions which prevail. But to many people it is a matter of conviction that the missionary battle is going to be lost or won on the witness of the layman, and on the emergence of dynamic centres of Christian community acting as leaven within the lump; and that this is true for any situation in which the Church is set. I can only record that, in many rural areas of Britain with which I have had personal contact in the work of evangelism, this approach to mission, if courageously and humbly undertaken, has yielded the most remarkable and far-reaching results.

It goes without saying that the mission of friendship can be carried out by a single congregation or by a group of churches acting together. In most small towns, indeed, it is desirable that the mission should be collective and inter-denominational, with parish boundaries which are largely fictitious swept aside in the interests of unity.

(iii) The Follow-Up

At the end of the first visitation, it has been said, the real work of the mission begins. Of one thing I am quite certain. Where a mission of this kind has not fulfilled expectations it has only been because the follow-up work has not been adequately done. In one sense the mission has only begun with the initial visitation.

Responsibility for immediate follow-up can be distributed among the various organizations of the church, according to the needs of the situation. Sunday school, uniformed movements, women's organizations, office-bearers, can all play their part. A large share of the burden of follow-up will inevitably fall on the minister, and for a considerable spell he will be required to rearrange his time-table to make room for this essential work.

It is impossible to write more about follow-up. These visits have to be continued over many months, and conform to no set pattern. And in a sense the follow-up is the prelude to a new and significant situation. For it confronts us with the supreme problem which I have tried to express in this book—how are the new members who come from the visitation to be absorbed into the existing fellowship? And yet, at the same time, it should bring us to the point of real discovery—namely, to the re-examination of the presuppositions on which our whole church life is based.

I have already analysed at some length the results which can be expected from a mission of this kind. There will be an immediate response seen in the accession of new members, and increased numbers in the various organizations. But these are by no means the most important results. The work will be ultimately effective if the group of volunteers becomes, through the reality of its experience in the mission, a true *koinonia*; if what began as a parish mission becomes, in effect, a missionary parish; and if the mission of friendship is a prelude to a constant mission of service. These things will not take place overnight. And they will cause upheaval within the Church. Dr. George Macleod has put it succinctly in his book, *We Shall Rebuild*: 'The one necessity is that the congregation be an organism and not a static Roll. It is only through an organism that a Living God can work.'

VII

THE MINISTRY IN A MISSIONARY PARISH

1. The Demands of the Ministry

PROFESSOR G. D. HENDERSON, in his book, *The Claims of the Church of Scotland*, quotes a saying of Richard Baxter: ' All Churches either rise or fall as the Ministry doth rise or fall.' I want in this last chapter to look specifically at the work of the minister in the kind of situation I have been trying to outline, with Baxter's dictum as the starting point. It reminds us of a truth which those of us who have been called to the ministry often find insupportable, and one from which we seek time and again to escape. Simply this: that the ultimate success or failure of a parish or congregation—in the deepest sense—depends on the quality of the ministry. The Commission of Evangelism appointed by the Archbishops of Canterbury and York put it plainly in their report, *Towards the Conversion of England*: ' If the Apostolate of the whole Church, clergy and laity alike, is to be recovered, if the Church itself is to become a weapon for evangelism, the clergy are, and must be, the key to the situation. The spiritual temperature of a congregation depends chiefly on the parish priest. That awful responsibility is his, and he cannot escape from it. Generally speaking, the Church cannot rise higher than the lives of its clergy . . . the parish priest

99

is the gift of the Ascended Christ to the Church " in order fully to equip his people for the work of serving —for the building up of Christ's Body ".'

Of course, it is something which many of us in the ministry do not care to admit; but that does not alter the truth of it. In the Scottish Churches Radio Mission of 1951-52 it was my privilege to visit many different parts of the country to enlist support for the mission, and bring to the microphone ministers and people from different parishes throughout Scotland who were engaged in the work of parochial evangelism. This fact emerged quite clearly—that wherever there was devoted ministerial leadership there was a group of lay people eager to respond, and a congregation alive to the real issues of Christian living. Where there was no such ministerial leadership, the eager goodwill of lay people for the idea of mission was dissipated and lost. I have written at length in this book about the lay apostolate. I believe that there are groups of laymen in all our churches who are prepared to undertake the hazardous and uncomfortable task of translating their faith into the concrete terms of daily life. But they need leadership and guidance. And that can only come from a ministry deeply aware of its responsibilities and courageously committed to the fulfilment of those obligations for which it was ordained.

In all this there is an obvious danger at which I have already hinted. True ministerial leadership should not be confused with the pernicious cult of the ' popular preacher ', which has done so much to undermine the real foundations of the Protestant ministry in the past hundred years, but which, fortunately, is beginning to die in our own time. As I hope to show in this chapter, ministerial leadership in its deepest sense is in fact only possible when the minister is most truly one with his people, their servant for Christ's sake, and realizing that the work of God in his parish is not his own exclusive responsibility but the corporate task of the community of which he is the representative.

What, then, are the demands laid upon the minister by his ordination? In his book, *A Manual of Church Doctrine*, H. J. Wotherspoon quotes this paragraph from the section on 'Pastors' in an old Form of Church Government: 'It belongs to the office of the minister to pray for and with his flock, as the mouth of the people unto God; to pray for the sick; to read the Scriptures publicly; to feed the flock by preaching the word; to catechize; to dispense other divine mysteries; to administer the Sacraments; to bless the people from God; to take care of the poor; and to rule.' It is a moving statement of the task of the ministry. But when I set it alongside the work which for the most part occupied my time and my attention in my own parish I am compelled to realize how disparate are the ideal and the reality. And when I am told, further, at my own ordination, that in addition to the pastoral care of the congregation committed to me I am also charged with the task of evangelism in the parish where my church stands, then I begin to despair at the absolute impossibility of facing the demands which are made upon me. I have tried to examine some of the issues involved in so far as they affect the congregation, and to trace some of the steps which might lead to the emergence of a missionary parish. If this is, in any sense, even the beginning of an answer to our fundamental problem, and if, in fact, so much depends on the minister himself, is it not evident that we have to ask ourselves two questions: What are the factors in our own situation which so often prevent us from exercising our ministry to the full? And secondly: How can we overcome these things and begin to break through the circle of our own ineffectiveness?

2. *Strangers to our own People?*

What are the factors in our own situation which so often prevent us from exercising our ministry to the full? It seems to me that there are at least five answers to this question, three of them obvious and in a sense superficial; two of them not so obvious, much more controversial, and in my judgment supremely important.

First of all, there is the simple fact of the shortage of clergy. The idea of a team-ministry is widely accepted in principle in the Church of Scotland. Over and over again it is canvassed as at least one solution to the parish problem. And on the face of it, the idea is reasonable. It is a sheer physical impossibility for one man to overtake the work involved in a congregation of perhaps a thousand members, set in a parish of ten thousand souls. If the responsibility could be divided among two or three men working together, if the work of the multifarious agencies of a modern church could be shared, then—theoretically at least—it would make for a more effective ministry. It is idle to talk of a team-ministry, however, so long as the man-power shortage in the Church is so increasingly acute. In the pre-war session of 1937-38, the number of Church of Scotland students in the divinity colleges was 322. In 1947-48, with the influx of post-war candi-

dates, the number was 210.   In the current session
(1952-53) some 37 students have entered the first year
of the four Church of Scotland colleges, and I am told
that the situation may become worse in the near future.
Exactly the same situation exists in the Anglican and
Free Churches in England.   It is no part of my purpose
at this stage to enquire into the reasons for the serious
decline in the number of candidates for the ministry.
I am simply concerned to point out that so long as this
shortage of clergy exists, the task of the ministry—*as
it is presently conceived*—is impossible to accomplish.

The second factor which contributes to the ineffectiveness of the parish minister in the fulfilment of his
real obligation is his enslavement to routine.   Professor
James Stewart in his Warrack lectures, *Heralds of God*,
writes: 'Beware the professional busy-ness which is
but slackness in disguise.   The trouble is that we may
even succeed in deceiving ourselves.   Our diary is
crowded.   Meetings, discussions, interviews, committees, throng the hectic page.   We are driven here, there,
everywhere by the whirling machinery of good works.
We become all things to all men.   Laziness?   The word,
we protest, is not in our vocabulary.   Are we not
engrossed from morning till night?   Do we not con-
spicuously spend our days under the high pressure of
an exacting life?'   No parish minister is unfamiliar with
this 'whirling machinery of good works'.   His life is
a perpetual struggle against overwhelming odds to get
through the formal routine of his vocation, and never
a day ends without his realization of something left
unattended.   If he works a sixteen-hour day he still
fails to overtake his commitments.   And in all this unending tyranny of routine the central things of his

calling have time and again to be sacrificed or carried through inadequately. His pulpit work is left to a Saturday, despite the lecturers on preaching who tell him that his mornings should be devoted to his study. His pastoral work is scamped in an unequal struggle to get through an impossible list of visits. His opportunities for instructing the young communicant—when they have not been completely omitted—are confined to a few fifteen-minute periods after the morning service. And this is true both for the city minister and for the minister in a rural area where the calls upon his time, if less obvious, are no less demanding.

The third factor which hampers and cripples our ministry is that so many of us are, in the wrong sense, servants of our people. We accept the judgment of our congregation on what constitutes an effective ministry, and either for the sake of peace, or because of our fear of failure on the human level, or even because of our fear of economic insecurity, we capitulate to that judgment. In this, one can only speak for oneself. In the congregation in which I minister, the vast majority of the members hold a clearly defined and simple view of the qualities which go to make a successful priest. He should be able to preach what they would call an 'acceptable' sermon—that is, one which is quiet, comfortable, 'spiritual', and unexacting. He should be a good mixer, as much at home at a club dance as he is in the pulpit, with a fund of racy stories for the social occasion. He should be—perhaps above all—a good 'visitor'; which means that he ought to be on the doorstep with unfailing regularity at least once or twice a year, and possess an occult power of divining exactly when he is required on all other occasions.

Given these things, a congregation will remain reasonably happy and reasonably uncritical. But should a man fail to interpret his vocation in this light, should he attempt to carry the wider demands of his calling into action, and look beyond the gathered flock to the needs of the teeming world outside, his troubles will begin. It is never easy to face conflict of this kind. And as often as not we become, not the servants of our people for Christ's sake, but their lackeys.

But these things are, as I have said, obvious and superficial. There are reasons much more profound for our failure to discharge fully the terms of our ordination and ' bless the people from God '.

The first is the inadequacy of our training for the ministry, on its pastoral side. I am not condemning the devoted teaching of those professors of pastoral theology in our divinity colleges, who do their utmost in the time at their disposal. What I am concerned to suggest is that far too little of our training for the ministry is directed towards equipping the ordinand to meet the practical realities of his work in a parish. It seems to me, for example, that at some point in his training the student should be sent to do his normal period of national service, or take a job for a spell in a factory or shipyard—although I agree with Professor G. D. Henderson when he writes that ' plenty of people work in offices and factories without seeming to learn anything very surprising, and a dabbler might easily develop a false confidence '. But that idea is not fundamentally important. It is much more important that the candidate for the ministry should be prepared as far as is humanly possible to deal not with a situation which existed fifty years ago, but with the situation as it exists to-day. At the moment our training is primarily academic, in the worst sense. There is no slick solution to the problem. But meanwhile it contributes at least to what appears to me to be the most fundamental of all the reasons for our ineffectiveness—namely, that we are separated from our people by what the Abbé Michonneau has called our 'clerical culture'.

I have mentioned Michonneau's book, *Revolution in a City Parish*, earlier. I have read nothing on the work of the ministry more exciting, stimulating and humiliating than this book. Of course it is not pleasant reading, for very few of us have the courage to face up to our own weakness, as Michonneau has done, and try to change it. He gives it as his opinion that the main reason for our failure to evangelize the people around us is our clerical culture, by which he means that 'our influence upon ordinary people is not what it should be partly because we are so different from them; we think differently, live differently, speak and act differently. In other words, we have a different culture. Our seminary training in the classics, philosophy and theology has put us in a class apart. Properly speaking we are not like any of our parishioners, but we seem more "middle-class" than anything else. What is the result? Usually it means that we feel compelled to surround ourselves with those who will understand our thought and speech, and who have tastes like our own . . . our priestly influence becomes narrower, and our priestly hearts become less catholic. . . . The heart of the difficulty lies in this, that we have enclosed ourselves in our own little clerical world, and that we have tried to make the outside world conform to that pattern. If it will not, we avoid contact with it; if it will, we feel that we are accomplishing something. The truth is that we have failed in the rôle of an *alter Christus* and are playing the part of an *alter ego*, dressed in clerical robes.'

The natural reaction to that paragraph is to deny its relevance for ourselves. We feel that it may be true of the priesthood in France, where the gulf between the Church and the world is so wide: but is it true of our own country? Again, one can only speak for oneself. While I find it comparatively easy to mix with the professional and middle-class people of my parish and speak to them of the Faith, I find it inexpressibly hard to establish the same relationship among what are called the working-classes, although I was born and brought up in a working-class home. It is not merely that there is a social gulf between us—although that exists, and is not consciously of my creating. It is exactly what Michonneau describes as a difference in culture. In an earlier chapter I have written about the secular culture pattern which characterizes the Church and separates it from the mass of the people— a culture pattern the chief marks of which are its respectability, its desire for self-perpetuation, its complacency, its introversions and allophoby. It is our subservience as ministers to this same culture pattern which makes it possible for us to play *alter ego* to one section of the community, which divides us from another, and which finally denies us the possibility of standing as an *alter Christus* to any man—which is our true vocation. In this sense, and for this reason above all, we are strangers to our own people.

3. The Minister and his Priorities

The second question we set ourselves to ask was this : How can we overcome these things, and break through the circle of our ineffectiveness? What steps can be taken to get away from the ' whirling machinery of good works'; to be true to our vocation, not as it is interpreted by our people, but as we know God meant it to be; and above all, to move among all men as one ' taken from among men and ordained for men in those things which have to do with the service of God '?

At the simplest level, it seems to me that we have to begin with a reassessment of our priorities as ministers. Again and again we have to remind ourselves of the terms of our vocation. The writer to the Ephesians speaks of the vocation of the Christian, and the supreme unity of the Church, which is the Body of Christ. He looks forward to the day when the mighty purpose of God will be fulfilled and we shall ' all come in the unity of the faith . . . unto a perfect man, unto the measure of the stature of the fulness of Christ '. Towards this great end we are to use the diversity of gifts that God has given the Church. ' And he gave some, apostles; and some, prophets; and some, evangelists; and some, pastors and teachers; for the perfecting of the saints, for the work of the ministry, for the edifying of the body of Christ.' Is it not, in fact, an image of the different aspects of our calling as ministers, reminding us of the nature of our vocation, and the things to which we are primarily committed?

An apostle is one who is sent, one who makes his dwelling among the people to whom he has been commissioned. And the minister has to begin there. If he is to bear witness to the mighty acts of God he must enter deeply into the life of the world, as Christ himself did in his incarnation. The minister must live alongside the people for whom Christ died, shirk no contact with the world, share with his people their burdens and perplexities and sorrows, and so share the fellowship of his Lord's suffering.

It must be a prophetic ministry. The prophet is supremely a man who sees into the heart of his own time and brings it under the judgment of the eternal. He is in the world, but not of it. He accepts no conventions, is bound by no human standards. At the risk of persecution and misunderstanding he proclaims his message over against all human values. So the minister must fulfil his prophetic task, bringing the whole of life under God's judgment, tearing aside the pretensions and shams and hypocrisies behind which the world seeks to hide itself from the searching light of God.

The minister must be an evangelist—presenting in its fulness the whole Gospel of God, leading men to Christ, their sole Saviour and Lord, and demanding a decision in his name. And this evangelism can only be effective when his apostolic and prophetic functions have been fulfilled. There is no evangelism, nor has there ever been, which did not drive the servants of God to the place where Christ has been—to the stark loneliness of Gethsemane, and the agony of a cross.

Finally, the minister is called to be pastor and teacher, caring for the souls of his people, leading them through the dark places, and instructing them in the faith once delivered to the saints.

In that remarkable book of Roman pastoral theology, *The People's Priest*, Bishop John C. Heenan writes:

'Look at the newly ordained priest. He has about him a certain aura . . . it is almost physical, though hard to describe. It is seen in the enthusiasm with which he discharges his priestly functions. His looks and demeanour show that he is charged with new spiritual vitality . . . the experienced priest might ask himself, Have I retained my early ambition? Do I still want God to make me a saint? Have I settled down to an unexacting way of life? I am well thought of by my parishioners. I still have my name in the Catholic Directory. . . . If ideals and ambitions have fallen so low I must say "*Non sum qualis eram!*"' We have to be led constantly to this recollection of our ordination —our identification with men; our proclamation of the Word of God; our winning men for Christ; our pastoral care of souls in the administering of the Sacraments and the instruction of the flock. For these things everything else must stand aside.

In practical terms these things make their own demands, and determine the spheres of our service. First of all, there is our preparation for public worship —the preaching of the Word, and the administration of the Sacraments. The Ministers' Fraternal of which J. H. Jowett was a member was discussing at one of its meetings the difficulty of studying and sermon preparation during the morning because of the continual interruption of telephone and door-bell. It was observed that Jowett had remained silent throughout the discussion; and when he was asked for his opinion he is reported to have said: 'My telephone never rings at six in the morning.' A counsel of perfection, perhaps. But one which we have to follow if our first duty is to be adequately discharged.

Second, there is our pastoral work. I have said something of the exacting requirements which a congregation can make upon their minister in the matter of visitation. Very few of our members have the remotest idea of what congregational visitation really involves. In my own congregation there are roughly eight hundred and fifty homes. If I spend three nights a week visiting these homes, giving three hours a night to it, and spending half an hour in each home, it will take me forty-seven weeks to complete the visitation. But no such calculation can in practice be made. The more we come to know our people the less is it possible—or desirable—to visit them with one eye on the clock. A single visit, if we are really going out on God's business, may occupy a whole evening. And unless our visiting is truly pastoral it is irrelevant. There is little virtue in seeing every member of our congregation once a year if our visit is spent in amiable conversation. It may raise us in the esteem of our people. But assuredly it is distracting us from the work of God.

Finally, there is our work of instruction and teaching. It is at this point that I feel we are most evidently failing, partly because this side of our work is neglected to make room for that ' whirling machinery of good works ', and partly because we are slow to recognize its potentialities. There are three areas of instruction which are of primary importance, and which no minister can afford to disregard. The first is the Sunday school; the second is the Confirmation class; and the third is provided by our occasional offices.

I feel that every minister ought to be Superintendent of his own Sunday school, despite the additional burden this will impose upon him on a day already overcrowded. Apart from anything else it gives him a close and intimate personal contact with the children of his parish which he can get in no other way. It allows him to supervise the training of his teachers and the curriculum of his school. Above all, he has a unique opportunity of guiding the minds of the children under his care, and leading them into ways of thought and ways of worship which it is infinitely hard to teach men and women whose habits of thought are settled and often immovable. One of the most satisfying things in the work of the ministry is to see children we have worked with over a period of years growing up to accept a view of the Faith radically different from the conventionalism of so much of the Church's life, and taking their place in the active work and witness of the Christian community. The missionary parish does not evolve overnight. It is the product of years of careful and patient labour. The work among children is one of its most important aspects.

The Confirmation class offers a no less fruitful field of instruction. It is a regrettable fact that in many congregations the Confirmation class is either non-existent or hopelessly inadequate. Theoretically, of course, there should be little need for a long period of instruction of young people coming into full member-ship of the Church when they have passed through Sunday school and Bible class. By the time they reach the age of seventeen or eighteen they should have received a thorough grounding in the Faith. But that remains only a theory. In my own congregation at least fifty per cent of those coming forward to member-ship by profession of faith since 1946 have been over thirty years of age, and the great majority of these have been men and women whose contact with the Church over the years has been casual and incidental. The minimum preparation they require is an extended course of instruction in the elementary facts of the Faith; and probably we would do well to think in terms of a probationary period before they are asked to come forward to full membership. The extraordinary ignorance of the Bible for example, which is characteristic of so many members of the Church, seems to me to be directly due to the cavalier fashion in which these people were received into membership in the Church. A cup of coffee and a friendly chat at the manse is not exactly an adequate preparation for first Communion.

The opportunities offered by the Confirmation class were brought home forcibly to me when, following the 1950 Churches-Radio Mission, I was asked to bring my class to a studio and broadcast a twelve-weeks course of instruction. The Rev. R. H. W. Falconer, Religious Broadcasting Organizer for Scotland, wrote in his book, *Success and Failure of a Radio Mission*, this account: ' I doubt if I have ever been more moved as a Christian minister than I was the first night I watched the group enter the studio which was to be our class-room in Broadcasting House, Glasgow. Here were normal church young people, yes, decent youngsters, rather overawed by what they were doing. But here were oldish women, wives and mothers with the marks of toil on face and hands, women who had been so busy rearing families and serving them, that somehow they have never got round to joining the Church. Here too were men: ex-servicemen in their late twenties and early thirties from the Army, the Navy, the R.A.F., of the type we covet greatly in the Church and seldom win; men who had faced life at its most terrifying and were now seeking the answer—one of them but recently out of prison. Here were students, budding teachers, and others, and, somewhat shyly, a few young couples, either recently married or about to be. Here were old and young, married and single, educated and uneducated, working-class and professional, and quite literally, "rich man, poor man, begger man, thief". A veritable cross-section of society from the bottom to the top; the people for whom Christ lived and died.' That particular Confirmation class is almost exactly typical of the group of people who have been coming forward to church membership since our first parish mission, usually between thirty and forty of them twice a year, won for the Church by the work of the ordinary members of the congregation seriously committed to the business of evangelism. Under Mr. Falconer's guidance, we began our course of instruction. What happened?

Again I quote Mr. Falconer: 'Lives were changed: under God, we saw it happening. They were changed on the human level, chiefly because of the astonishing honesty of it all. No question was side-stepped, and questions were two-way in flow . . . here was the *dynamic* with which the Christian fellowship should be possessed but which we experience so seldom. . . . We were privileged to share in the powerful, questing, disconcerting, all-mighty dynamic of Christ his Spirit.'

The class of Confirmation was an unforgettable experience. It taught us that men and women are thirsting for positive instruction. It provided the pattern for the congregational group which subsequently emerged. Here is a priority which cannot be set aside by a minister without infinite loss.

I suggested that the third significant field of instruction is provided by the 'occasional offices' which we are asked to perform. Every parish minister is familiar with the constant demands made upon his time by those people, claiming no church connection, who come to ask for his services in baptisms, marriages, and burials. Our natural response to these requests is to carry them through as an additional duty which only helps to distract us from the clamouring things within our church demanding our attention. And yet these occasional offices are by far our most significant opportunities for personal evangelism in its truest sense. In our discharge of them we are coming into contact with men and women whom we see at no other time, and at one of the great crises of life when mind and heart are most open to eternal things. At the risk of sacrificing something from our routine, we have to use these opportunities, not for the perfunctory performance of a formal service, but for positive instruction. An interview with parents seeking baptism for their child, or with a young couple about to be married, or a visit to a home recently bereaved can become the means of leading these people into the fellowship of the Church. It takes time. But it is a priority.

4. The Minister and the Group

I have said earlier in this chapter that ministerial leadership in its deepest sense is only possible when the minister realizes that the work of God in his parish is not his own exclusive responsibility, but the corporate task of the community of which he is the representative. I become increasingly certain that this is the key not only to an effective ministry, but to a genuine stirring of dynamic life within a congregation and parish. No one man can discharge the duties laid upon him, no matter how rigorously he tries to maintain a true sense of priority. Nor was he intended to. There are vast areas of the Church's work—particularly in evangelism and in pastoral care—which are the responsibility of the lay members of the Church, acting under the minister's guidance. When this becomes a reality within a congregation, the minister discovers that he is, in fact, part of a team ministry, with an instructed, devoted and disciplined laity as his assistants. Theoretically in the Church of Scotland the eldership should be performing this function. In practice, it is not. We cannot wait until our whole body of elders is alive to its responsibility. We have within our congregations men and women and young people who are prepared to make their membership of the Body of Christ a reality. And—as I have tried so inadequately in this book to show—with these people lies the future of the Church.

Daniel Jenkins, in his book, *The Gift of the Ministry*, writes this tremendous passage on the minister's calling, with which I want to end. When we can absorb its truth into our being we might begin to speak as 'the mouth of the people unto God, and bless the people from God'. Mr. Jenkins writes: 'All the doubts and difficulties and terrors which confront mortal men as they face the temptations and hazards and ambiguities of existence should be his familiar ground. Life at its grimmest and harshest should have an almost morbid fascination for him. Wherever there is trouble he should be found. He is the one man among all men who cannot be permitted the luxury of a sheltered life. . . . Like Lear, he must experience humiliation and agony and the storm before he is ready to be one of God's spies and seek out the mystery of things. . . . Like Abraham he must know what it means to lift the knife against Isaac his well-beloved son at the commandment of God, and like Paul he must be prepared to wish himself accursed for his brethren's sake. . . . Of all men, he has to be the freest thinker, allowing the most dangerous of facts to lead him wherever they will, without regard to personal safety or comfort or professional prestige, offering himself on the altar of God's truth, that God's glory might be made manifest in his weakness.'

Then, at last, we might behold the face of our parish and hear its voice, and know the supreme joy of seeing it become a living cell in the everlasting Church.

INDEX

DATE DUE

6. 09.83	